Vocabulary
in practice 6

40 units of
self-study
vocabulary
exercises

Liz Driscoll

with tests

CAMBRIDGE
UNIVERSITY PRESS

CAMBRIDGE UNIVERSITY PRESS
Cambridge, New York, Melbourne, Madrid, Cape Town, Singapore, São Paulo, Delhi

Cambridge University Press
The Edinburgh Building, Cambridge CB2 8RU, UK

www.cambridge.org
Information on this title: www.cambridge.org/9780521601269

First published 2005
3rd printing 2008

Printed in Dubai by Oriental Press

A catalogue record for this publication is available from the British Library

ISBN 978-0-521-60126-9 paperback

Contents

To the student

This book will give you the chance to practise your vocabulary in a fun way.

Vocabulary in Practice 6 has:

- 40 units of short, enjoyable exercises – each unit practises groups of words which belong together
- 4 Tests – one after every 10 units, helping you to remember the words from those units
- an Answer Key
- a Word List – this is a list of all the words in each unit with information about how the words are used.

You can use the book in two ways:

1 Start at the beginning of the book. Do units 1–40 and then do the Tests.
2 Look at the Contents. Do the units you think are important first. When you have finished the book, do the Tests.

You can do each unit in two ways:

1 Do the unit and check your answers in the Answer Key. Study the Word List and learn the words you got wrong. Then do the exercise again.
2 Study the Word List for the unit. Then do the unit and check your answers.

Note Do the exercises in this book in pencil. Then you can do the exercises again after a week or a month. Repeating the exercises will help you to remember the words.

Here are some ideas to help you to learn vocabulary:

- Write new words in a notebook: write the meaning in English or in your own language, then write a sentence using the word.
- List other related words: noun, verb, adjective [e.g. assertiveness/assert/ assertive].
- Write the words in phrases, not in isolation: adjectives with nouns [e.g. immediate family], verbs with nouns [e.g. make a promise], words with prepositions [e.g. related to].
- Note anything particular about grammar [e.g. irregular verb form] or usage [e.g. slim (positive), skinny (negative)].
- List words in groups: words with opposite meanings [e.g. extrovert/introvert, make money / lose money], words with similar meanings [e.g. relation/relative, run-down/shabby].

I hope you find this book useful and that it makes learning English words fun.

1 Describing character

A Match the beginnings and endings of the words to make nouns. Write the words.

1	confid	ity	_confidence_
2	consider	iasm	
3	court	ation	
4	creativ	ty	
5	enthus	ative	
6	flexib	~~ence~~	
7	initi	ility	
8	loyal	esy	

B Write the noun endings of these words. Use some of the endings from A.

1 determin............

2 hones............

3 independ............

4 intellig............

5 matur............

6 original............

7 pati............

8 reliab............

C What are these people like? Use the adjective form of words from A and B.

1 He takes into account other people's feelings.

2 She's polite and pleasant, and respects other people.

3 He likes working on his own.

4 He uses his imagination when he does new things.

5 She's always very interested in what she's doing.

6 He's willing to change his ideas if he has to.

7 She's very certain of her own abilities.

8 He always remains calm and doesn't get angry.

9 She always tells the truth.

10 She's supportive and doesn't change her beliefs.

11 He does his work in a sensible, adult way.

12 She always does what she says she'll do.

13 He always succeeds, though it's sometimes hard.

14 She's always different in her ideas from other people.

2 Describing appearance

A Complete the sentences with the words in the box.

crumpled   dowdy   fashionable   flattering
neat   old-fashioned   stylish   unflattering

If your clothes are:

1 .... , they are not modern.
2 .... , they are popular at a particular time.
3 .... , they are tidy and ordered with everything in its place.
4 .... , they are unattractive and not smart, often because they are old-fashioned.
5 .... , they make you look more attractive than you are.
6 .... , they are full of irregular folds.
7 .... , they are fashionable and smart.
8 .... , they make you look less attractive than you are.

B Replace the underlined words with the words in the box.

clean-cut   elegant   frumpy   glamorous   immaculate
nerdy   over-dressed   under-dressed

1 Sometimes at parties, people are <u>too formal or smart</u>. ....
2 My grandmother is very <u>graceful and attractive</u>. ....
3 The new chairman is very <u>clean, neat and tidy</u>. ....
4 Middle-aged women can look <u>old-fashioned and boring</u>. ....
5 My boss's wife always looks <u>perfectly clean and tidy</u>. ....
6 Hollywood actresses are usually <u>attractive and exciting</u>. ....
7 Sometimes clever people are <u>unattractive and boring</u>. ....
8 At the wedding, I was <u>not attractive or formal enough</u>. ....

C Put the words from A and B into the correct group.

positive		negative	
....	....	....	....
....	....	....	....
....	....	....	....
....	....	....	....

3 What your body does

A Find twelve verbs in the grid which you can use to describe what your body does. Write the words.

1 a _ _ _
2 b _ _ _
3 b _ _ _ _
4 h _ _ _ _ _
5 i _ _ _
6 s h _ _ _ _

7 s n _ _ _ _ _
8 s n _ _ _
9 s w _ _ _
10 t _ _ _ _
11 t _ _ _ _ _
12 y _ _ _

s	a	c	s	n	i	f	f	h	t
n	s	b	h	y	t	y	b	i	i
e	w	l	i	a	c	h	e	c	n
e	e	u	v	w	h	x	o	c	g
z	a	s	e	n	t	l	n	u	l
e	t	h	r	o	b	u	r	p	e

B Complete the sentences with verbs from A.

1 You can _____ when you're embarrassed about something.
2 You can _____ when you're cold or frightened.
3 You can _____ when you're hot, ill or frightened.
4 You can _____ when you have spots.
5 You can _____ when you're tired or bored.
6 You can _____ when you have a cold or are crying.

C Complete each sentence with one expression from both boxes.

can pop	when you're excited
can rumble	when you cut up onions
can beat fast	when you go up in a plane
can run	when you have a cold
can water	when you're hungry

1 Your nose _____
2 Your heart _____
3 Your eyes _____
4 Your stomach _____
5 Your ears _____

4 How you feel

A Circle the correct words to complete the sentences.

1 What's wrong? You seem very <u>apprehensive / edgy</u> today. Have you had an argument with someone?

2 My mum feels <u>settled / uncomfortable</u> when she sees my dad with his new wife.

3 Although he looked calm, he was actually feeling very <u>composed / tense</u>.

4 I began to feel <u>distracted / uneasy</u> when my sister wasn't home by midnight.

5 My aunt gets <u>anxious / expectant</u> when she's on her own in the house.

6 I get rather <u>jumpy / restless</u> when I'm in a car. I'm a bit of a nervous passenger.

B Complete the sentences with the other words from A.

1 I'm sure the speaker was nervous, but she looked very ....

2 I knew he wasn't listening to me – he was completely ....

3 My little nephew gets very .... if he can't go out to play.

4 I'm a bit .... about my dentist's appointment.

5 After six months, I finally feel .... in my job.

6 She looked very .... when I called her into my office. I think she was hoping for a pay rise.

C Circle the correct word for each definition.

1 happy because you are familiar with something   composed / settled / tense

2 excited because something interesting might happen   edgy / expectant / restless

3 nervous, anxious, especially because of fear or guilt   jumpy / settled / uncomfortable

4 fearful that something unpleasant is going to happen   apprehensive / restless / settled

5 worried, embarrassed; not relaxed and confident   distracted / expectant / uncomfortable

6 afraid, nervous or worried   anxious / composed / tense

7 unable to concentrate because you are thinking about something else   apprehensive / distracted / uncomfortable

8 anxious that something may be wrong   distracted / jumpy / uneasy

9 nervous, not relaxed, likely to lose control   edgy / expectant / uneasy

10 calm and controlled   anxious / apprehensive / composed

5 Animal types

A Complete the text with the words in the box.

amphibians	carnivores	domestic	endangered	herbivores	
human	insects	invertebrates	mammals	omnivores	pet
predator	prey	rare	reptiles	species	vertebrates	wild

There are well over one million different (1) .... of animal.
Almost all animals, including (2) .... , jellyfish and worms are
(3) .... – they have no backbone. There are five groups of
(4) .... :

- fish;
- birds;
- (5) .... , such as frog, newt;
- (6) .... , such as crocodile, snake;
- (7) .... , such as elephant, whale.

Some animals, such as elephants, eat plants and are called (8) .... Most
(9) .... animals, such as cows and sheep, eat only plants. Other animals,
such as cats, seals and tigers, are (10) .... – they feed on the flesh of
other animals. (11) .... dogs belong in this category. They hunt for food,
while our (12) .... dogs usually eat meat from a tin. (An animal that is a
(13) .... on other animals may, in turn, become
(14) .... to other larger animals.) Some animals, such as pigs, eat both
plants and flesh, and are therefore (15) ....

The reason that some (16) .... animals have become
(17) .... and even extinct is because their food source has disappeared –
either naturally or through (18) .... interference.

B Look at the photos. Which words from B can you use to describe these animals? Use the singular form of some of the words.

crocodile

....
....
....
....
....

horse

....
....
....
....

6 Working and not working

A Circle the correct words to complete the text.

I work in a food-processing factory. Most of the work is done during the day, but I work the night (1) <u>part-time job / shift</u> because the pay is better. My (2) <u>maternity leave / working hours</u> are from ten at night until six in the morning. I have to (3) <u>clock on / knock off</u> when I get there and (4) <u>clock off / take time off</u> before I go home. If you want some extra money, then there's sometimes some (5) <u>holiday allowance / overtime</u> available. If you do this, you don't finish work until about nine. But there's no (6) <u>flexitime / sick leave</u> here – if you don't work, you don't get paid. In fact, you can have a (7) <u>day off / lunch break</u> when you like – but you can't make a living that way. And if there's no work, you might (8) <u>get the sack / take early retirement</u>. Then you'd have to look for something else.

B Complete the text with the other words from A.

I work in the accounts office of a department store. We work a seven-and-a-half hour day with an hour's (1) .... The management is thinking of introducing (2) .... – then you could start work early in the day and (3) .... earlier too. It would also mean that we wouldn't have to (4) .... if we had to go to the doctor's or dentist's. We get 23 days' (5) .... a year. I've already had a long holiday in South Africa this year, but I've still got a few days left. Also, women can have six months' (6) ....,but I'm a bit young to be thinking of having children yet. In theory, we have to work until we're 65, but I'd much prefer to (7) .... because there are lots of things I'd rather do than work! Alternatively, I could get a (8) .... and work fewer hours every week.

C Circle the person who is more likely to do each thing.

1 have a longer holiday allowance – a teacher or a factory worker

2 work shifts – a gardener or a nurse

3 work flexitime – an office worker or a teacher

4 knock off at 5.30 – a shop assistant or a waiter

5 get paid overtime – a teacher or a mechanic

6 take maternity leave – a waiter or a waitress

7 Early childhood

A Label the items with the words in the box.

| bib   cot   dummy   high chair |
| nappy   pram   pushchair |

1 ....

2 ....

3 ....

4 ....

5 ....

6 ....

7 ....

B Complete the text with the words in the box and some of the words from A.

| babysitter   childminder   nursery   playground   pocket money |
| pre-school   teething   thumb |

My mum worked during my (1) .... years, so she wasn't the only person who looked after me when I was little. For the first three years of my life, Mum dropped me off every morning at the home of a (2) .... who I called Auntie Rita. So it was Auntie Rita who changed my (3) .... when it was dirty and smelly, and saw me through (4) .... and other childhood problems. Mum didn't want me to have a (5) .... when I cried, so that's probably when I started to suck my (6) .... Auntie Rita had a fold-up (7) .... in a downstairs cupboard, and every afternoon she pushed me to the local (8) .... , where she pushed me on the swings and roundabout. When I was three years old, I was old enough to go to a (9) .... The thing I liked most about it was that I didn't have to sit in a (10) .... for my meals. Even though I didn't see her every day, I didn't lose contact with Auntie Rita – when Mum was looking for a (11) .... so that she could go out in the evening, Auntie Rita's daughter said she would do it. And when I started to get (12) .... , the first thing I bought was some chocolate for the two of them.

C Write two words from A and B.

1 two things you can suck   .... , ...

2 two people you can stay with   .... , ...

3 two things you can lie down in   .... , ...

4 two places you can go to   .... , ...

5 two things you can wear   .... , ...

8 Friends and relationships

A Match the pairs of sentences. Write the letters in the box below.

1 I have a large circle of friends.
2 Bill was a friend of a friend.
3 Jane and I were childhood sweethearts.
4 Lola is an old friend of mine.
5 I was never part of a clique.
6 I met the twins through a mutual friend.

a She's been my pen pal since 1990.
b And now she's my fiancée.
c They'd been to the same school as me, although we weren't peers.
d I knew lots of different people.
e And now he's my flatmate.
f But Katy is the only school friend I have.

| 1 .... | 2 .... | 3 .... | 4 .... | 5 .... | 6 .... |

B Put the sentences in order to make the first part of the story. Write numbers in the boxes.

a They soon discovered that they had a lot in common – they both liked sport and travel. ☐

b Carrie got on with his parents too and they became close, perhaps because her own parents lived in Canada. ☐

c We used to hang around together sometimes after work. ☐

d About five years ago, I made friends with a girl at work called Carrie. ⑦

e Jim got to know them when he was working there. ☐

f One day I introduced her to my brother Jim. ☐

C Put the sentence endings in order to complete the second part of the story. Write the letters in the boxes.

1 However, because Jim worked abroad so much, ⑯
2 She also used to spend a lot of time with a male colleague of ours, ☐
3 When Jim and Carrie split up last year, ☐
4 We'd worked together for four years, after all, ☐
5 She's on speaking terms with Jim now, ☐
6 He needn't have worried about our male colleague, ☐

a she and I kept in touch for a while.
b but nothing more.
c and had been good friends.
d even though she told Jim they were 'just good friends'.
e since Carrie lost contact with him when the company closed down six months ago.
f he and Carrie grew apart.

9 Being good or bad

A Do the adjectives in *italics* mean 'good' (G) or 'bad' (B)? Write the letter next to each sentence.

1 The new secretary is very *efficient*. The office is much more organised now. ....

2 You'll be the only person in the shop. So you must be *capable* of working on your own. ....

3 I tried windsurfing, but I was absolutely *useless*. I spent more time in the water than on the board. ....

4 The president is an *effective* public speaker. People take notice of what he says. ....

5 My cousin is a *proficient* German speaker. He's lived in Berlin for the past eight years. ....

B Match the pairs of sentences. Write the letters in the box below.

1 My brother's very clumsy.
2 Ben's quite a competent swimmer.
3 Tony's totally inept at sport.

4 Paul's hopeless at reading maps.
5 John's quite skilful with his hands.

a Imagine him playing football!
b Don't ask him how to get there.
c He learnt when he was very young.
d He'll mend the window.
e He's always dropping things.

| 1 .... | 2 .... | 3 .... | 4 .... | 5 .... |

C Make a list of the adjectives in B. Do the adjectives mean 'good' (G) or 'bad' (B)?

1 ....
2 ....
3 ....
4 ....
5 ....

10 How you say something

A Put the letters in order to find ten verbs that describe what you are doing when you say something.

1 e g b   ....

2 f n s o e c s   ....

3 i r c o f n m   ....

4 m n d d a e   ....

5 i s n t s i   ....

6 t c i n r s u t   ....

7 p r t e o r   ....

8 q s e r u e t   ....

9 a r w e s   ....

10 r e u g   ....

B Complete the sentences in reported speech with the past simple form of verbs 1–5 from A.

1 'You really must stay the night, John,' she said. 'I won't let you go home.'

   She .... that John stay the night.

2 'Yes, my name is Fiona and I am nineteen years old,' she said.

   She .... that her name was Fiona and she was nineteen years old.

3 'Free all political prisoners!' they said.

   They .... that all political prisoners be freed.

4 'Please, please help me with the party, Charles,' she said.

   She .... Charles to help her with the party.

5 'I lied to the police,' he said.

   He .... that he had lied to the police.

C Rewrite the sentences in reported speech with the past simple form of verbs 6–10 from A.

1 'Go straight back to the office, Mrs Harris,' Gary said.

   ....

2 'It wasn't me,' he said. 'Honestly, it wasn't me.'

   ....

3 'Could you send me an email, Paul,' she said.

   ....

4 'Steve, don't drink and drive,' he said. 'You know it's not sensible.'

   ....

5 'There has been a sharp increase in drug-related crime,' the police said.

   ....

A **Complete the conversation. Write one word in each space.**

A: How do you manage with a baby and your work?

B: Well, I had six months' maternity (1) .... when he was born. And now I have a (2) .... job, so I only work five hours a day.

A: Who looks after the baby when you're at work?

B: I take him to a (3) .... every morning. She lives near us and she's very good at feeding him and changing his (4) .... when it's dirty.

A: What happens when he's sick?

B: Well, he's (5) .... at the moment, so he's crying a lot. I took time (6) .... last week because I didn't want to leave him.

A: What does your boss say?

B: She knows I often work through my lunch (7) .... , so she's fine about it. If necessary, I can use some of my holiday (8) ....

A: Does your husband help much?

B: Well, he's doing a lot of (9) .... at the moment because we want to buy a house. He's working long hours and sometimes he doesn't (10) .... off until about ten at night.

B **Look at the jumbled letters. Find two adjectives and write them in the table. The letters are already in order.**

	character	appearance
1 d o d e t w e r m d i n y e d	....	....
2 h e l o e n g e a n t s t	....	....
3 i l m m o a c y u a l l a t e	....	....
4 f f r l u e x m i b p l e y	....	....
5 r e n l e i a b a l e t	....	....
6 g l c r a e a m t o r i o v e u s	....	....

C **Circle two words for each animal.**

1 predator / reptile / wild

2 amphibian / human / vertebrate

3 domestic / herbivore / rare

4 endangered / invertebrate / mammal

Test 1 (Units 1–10)

D Are these sentences true or false?

1 An old friend is someone you lost contact with a long time ago. ....

2 Childhood sweethearts can grow apart as they get older. ....

3 You and your fiancé are 'just good friends'. ....

4 A mutual friend is someone you have a lot in common with. ....

5 A clique is a small group of friends who spend all their time together. ....

6 You keep in touch with your pen pal by writing to each other. ....

E The underlined words are in the wrong sentences. Write the correct word for each sentence.

1 I felt very useless about getting my exam results. ....

2 I've lived here for six years, so I feel clumsy. ....

3 What's on your mind? You seem very settled. ....

4 Be careful with that vase! You know how capable you are. ....

5 My aunt is nearly ninety, but she's still apprehensive of looking after herself. ....

6 I can't draw at all. I'm absolutely distracted. ....

F Circle the correct words to complete the sentences.

1 My ears popped / rumbled when the plane started to descend.

2 When the boss praised Caroline, she blushed / sweated with embarrassment.

3 I thought my brother had done it, but he begged / swore he hadn't.

4 The crowd instructed / urged the athletes to run faster.

5 When I went to university, I kept / lost contact with many of my school friends.

6 Shona grew / hung around with a small circle of friends.

7 I ached / itched all over after I'd been horse riding. I couldn't walk properly for a week.

8 My heart beat / ran very fast as I opened the envelope.

9 My mother demanded / insisted on paying for lunch.

10 The travel agent phoned and confessed / confirmed all our flight details.

11 Reactions

A Match the sentence halves. Write the letters in the box below.

1 The audience didn't greet
2 Today's announcement is likely to
3 The newspaper editor won't reply
4 Students are likely to react
5 The prime minister didn't respond
6 Car users may overreact

a to the new parking prices.
b the news enthusiastically.
c to the crisis soon enough.
d provoke strike action.
e to our letter personally.
f angrily to the fee increases.

1	2	3	4	5	6

B Circle the correct words to complete the newspaper extracts.

1 The public's response to the increase in fuel prices has been one of <u>outrage / welcome</u>.

2 The council's decision to abolish parking meters has been given the <u>backlash / thumbs up</u> by car users in the city.

3 The crowd was filled with <u>astonishment / dismay</u> when it started to rain during the air display.

4 The defection of the minister to the opposition party is being greeted with <u>outcry / suspicion</u>.

5 The audience loved the show and responded with great <u>delight / shock</u>.

6 The actor expressed <u>amazement / condemnation</u> at winning his third Oscar.

C Complete the newspaper extracts with the other words from B.

1

victory. The ....
over the council's plans has led
them to reconsider the location of
the new prison. Meanwhile, local

2

local supermarket. The price
cuts were given a warm
.... when they
were introduced a month ago.

3

partner of many years. No-one
expected the couple to get
married, so the news was
greeted with ....

4

since last Thursday. The kidnapping
of the small child has received
nationwide ....

5

Neighbours say that the
pensioner never recovered from
the .... of a
recent burglary. She lived in

6

empty. The closure of the factory
has provoked a ....
in a community that already has high
unemployment. Former workers

12 Opinions: for and against

A Circle the correct words to complete the sentences.

1 I've always been anti-smoking, so I approve / object of the new ban on smoking in public places.

2 I'm behind / undecided which way to vote. I haven't made up my mind about it yet.

3 Mum and Dad always back / oppose me, whatever I do. They want me to succeed.

4 People usually sympathise / take sides with the Democrats, but they're not willing to support them on this issue.

5 I know someone who's a member of a pro-nuclear group. He's in agreement / in favour of nuclear weapons, but I don't think they're a good thing.

6 Did the minister advocate / disapprove the building of a further motorway? He usually speaks in favour of more roads.

B Complete the sentences with the other words from A.

1 Most people are .... the government in their determination to reduce crime.

2 My parents .... of what I'm doing. They feel it's wrong.

3 Some people don't want to .... when there's an argument between two opposing groups.

4 We .... to the new parking charges. We've expressed our disapproval many times.

5 I'm .... with my neighbours about the new streetlights. We all have the same opinion.

6 Our MP said he would .... the new bill. He would speak against it in Parliament.

C Which words in A mean that you are 'for' something? Which words mean that you are 'against'?

for   against

....

....

....

....

13 Talking about history

A Complete the sentences with the words in the boxes.

1 My grandparents collect .... furniture.

2 In .... times, women didn't wear trousers.

3 We visited some .... temples in Mexico.

| ancient |
| antique |
| bygone |

4 His most famous .... was the first king.

5 The .... to the throne was the queen's nephew.

6 I'm a direct .... of the first family to come here.

| ancestor |
| descendant |
| heir |

7 Britain was in the Roman .... for about 400 years.

8 Many people moved abroad in the post-war ....

9 The television was invented during the last ....

| century |
| empire |
| era |

10 Discoveries of bones tell us about human ....

11 Few people in my grandparents' .... had cars.

12 Education was an important part of Greek ....

| civilisation |
| evolution |
| generation |

13 The earliest .... people lived in East Africa.

14 Many big churches were built in .... Europe.

15 Some Shakespeare plays are based on .... events.

| historical |
| medieval |
| prehistoric |

B Match the words from A with the definitions.

1 period of 100 years ....

2 relative who lived a long time ago ....

3 of the time before history was written down ....

4 belonging to or connected with the distant past ....

5 group of countries ruled by one person ....

6 unusual and valuable because it is old and rare ....

7 society with highly developed culture and way of life ....

8 of the period from 1100 to 1500 AD ....

9 process of change and development ....

10 people who were born about the same time ....

11 person who gets money or title when someone dies ....

12 period of time that is special for some reason ....

13 connected with history or the study of history ....

14 happening or existing in the past ....

15 person who is related to someone who lived a long time ago ....

14 The rich and famous

A Write the names of the TV programmes in the schedule.

> At home in the Caribbean   The Simon Smith Show
> Harvard House Hotel   They haven't always been famous
> Rebel Without a Cause

8.00 ....
This week's celebrity is Marie Paul, renowned for her marriages as much as her singing. We chart her rise to fame from those early days in Newcastle to her current status as a household name.

8.30 ....
Charlie Smith is a self-made millionaire with a luxury lifestyle and VIP neighbours. We visit him in his mansion on the island of Martinique.

9.00 ....
Guests arrive by limousine and are treated to the red carpet throughout their two-day stay at the health and beauty spa. As cameras roll, it seems that some of them love to be in the public eye!

9.30 ....
Our host chats to world-famous sports personality Neil Ramsay and star of daytime TV Tessa Jordan about life in the limelight.

10.00 ....
(Nicholas Ray, 1955)
The best teen movie yet, starring James Dean as a misunderstood youngster. Released after the death of the teen icon in a car crash earlier that year.

B Look at the schedule again. Answer the questions.

1 Marie Paul is a *celebrity*. Find two other words which have a similar meaning.

2 The adjective *renowned* means 'famous'. Find two expressions which mean 'very famous'.

3 Which expression means 'becoming famous'?

4 Which word for a person refers to the amount of money they have?

5 Which two words are *luxury* items?

6 *VIP* treatment is 'special treatment'. Find another expression with the same meaning.

7 Which two expressions mean 'in the centre of media and public attention'?

8 Which word means 'a famous person who represents a particular idea or a way of life'?

15 Cultures

A Circle the correct words to complete the first part of the text.

The word (1) <u>aborigine / discrimination</u> comes from the Latin *ab origine* meaning 'from the beginning'. It is used to mean any (2) <u>indigenous / westernised</u> inhabitant of a country nowadays. The Aborigines probably moved southwards from Asia to Australia, island-hopping in their canoes. They spread over the country in large family groups, or (3) <u>civil rights / tribes</u>, each with its own language and (4) <u>customs / ethnic groups</u>. They all tried to live in harmony with the land, which they worshipped because, according to their (5) <u>folklore / way of life</u>, the spirits of their ancestors had created its features back in a period they called the Dreamtime. European (6) <u>cultural identity / settlement</u> in Australia began around 200 years ago, and there were immediate conflicts with the (7) <u>multicultural / native</u> population. Their (8) <u>heritage / traditional</u> weapons, spears and boomerangs, were no match for guns.

B Use the other words from A to complete the second part of the text.

The Aboriginal (1) _____ has changed enormously since the Europeans arrived. Many Aborigines have now become more (2) _____ and live in big cities. Indeed, Australia is very much a (3) _____ society, and today the Aborigines are only one of many (4) _____ . In recent years, there has been a movement for the recognition of their (5) _____ , campaigning against (6) _____ in housing, education, wages and inadequate medical facilities. Some of them work hard to maintain their (7) _____ , so that the younger generation can learn about the traditions of the past and other aspects of their (8) _____ .

16 Body language

A The <u>underlined</u> words are in the wrong sentences. Write the correct word for each sentence.

1 If you <u>slouch</u>, you make continuous small movements which annoy other people. ....

2 If you <u>grimace</u>, you stand, sit or walk with the head bent slightly over and the shoulders hanging forward. ....

3 If you <u>tut</u>, you make your body or part of your body straighter and longer. ....

4 If you <u>fidget</u>, you put your tongue behind your teeth and suck in air in order to show your disapproval or annoyance. ....

5 If you <u>stretch</u>, you make a deep breath that can be heard. ....

6 If you <u>sigh</u>, you twist your face in an ugly way. ....

B Complete each sentence with one word from both boxes.

clench cross raise shrug lick fold	arms eyebrows legs lips shoulders teeth

1 If you .... your .... , you put one knee on top of the other.

2 If you .... your .... , you move the top of your face upwards.

3 If you .... your .... , you move your tongue along them.

4 If you .... your .... , you hold them together close to your chest.

5 If you .... your .... , you close your mouth very tightly.

6 If you .... your .... , you raise them and then lower them.

C Circle the gesture which is more likely to show each thing.

1 pain – grimace / stretch

2 surprise – raise your eyebrows / shrug your shoulders

3 sadness – fidget / sigh

4 anger – clench your teeth / sigh

5 disapproval – slouch / tut

6 tiredness – lick your lips / slouch

7 lack of interest or care – shrug your shoulders / tut

8 nervousness – fidget / raise your eyebrows

9 tiredness – stretch / clench your teeth

10 pleasure at the thought of food – grimace / lick your lips

17 Humour

A **Find two words and match them with the definitions. The letters of the words are already in order.**

1 ~~j~~ w ~~o~~ ~~k~~ i ~~e~~ t
   a a funny story, which is told to make you laugh   *joke*
   b the ability to use words in a clever and amusing way

2 b l a d c r k y
   a humour that is funny in a cruel or unpleasant way
   b humour that is very amusing although it sounds serious

3 s p a t u i r n e
   a an amusing use of a word with two meanings
   b the use of humour to attack someone or something that you think is bad or foolish

4 p i u n r c h o l i n n y e
   a a way of speaking that shows you mean the opposite of what you say
   b the last and most important words in a joke or funny story

B **Match the sentence halves. Write the letters in the box below.**

1 If you have a laugh about something,
a you make a type of joke with a word which has two meanings.

2 If you do something for a laugh,
b you tell them something that is not true as a way of joking with them.

3 If you make fun of someone,
c you do it for amusement.

4 If you use a play on words,
d you say it as a joke, although you might seem to be serious.

5 If you say something tongue in cheek,
e you make a joke about them in an unkind way.

6 If you tease someone,
f you see the funny side of it even though it was at first rather upsetting.

7 If you pull someone's leg,
g you laugh at, annoy or embarrass them.

1	2	3	4	5	6	7

18 Drugs

A Put twelve of the words in the box into three groups.

abuse	addiction	be	clean	dealer	fix	habit	~~hard~~
be high	be hooked	junkie	overdose	soft	take	trafficking

D R U G

D R U G S ..... *hard* .....

D R U G S

B Match the three other words from A with the definitions.

1 someone who takes and is dependent on drugs ....

2 amount of a drug which has an effect on someone ....

3 free from or cured from addiction to drugs ....

C Complete the text with words from A and B.

Radio One, 10.00 pm
Other people's lives – David, drug addict

David Duncan has been (1) .... on drugs since the age of sixteen.

He tells *Other people's lives* how he started with (2) .... drugs when

he was at school and then moved on to heroin. David's best friend Pete used to

be a (3) .... too – a (4) .... who lived nearby sold

them their daily (5) .... , which they injected, sometimes into each

other. But since Pete died of a heroin (6) .... , David has been

desperate to rid himself of his (7) .... Will David manage to get

(8) .... , and stay that way? Listen in and find out.

19 Medical treatment

Match the <u>underlined</u> words with the definitions below.

We've had a bad year in my family this year. First of all, my granddad was rushed into hospital by <u>ambulance</u> with pains in his chest. He had suffered a heart attack and was put on a <u>life-support machine</u> to keep his heart beating. In the end, he needed a <u>transplant</u>. The <u>operation</u> took more than ten hours. He was then in <u>intensive care</u> for four weeks before being allowed home. He's much better now, although he'll be on <u>medication</u> for the rest of his life.

Soon after that, my cousin was in a serious car crash. The first person on the scene had done some <u>first aid</u> and knew you shouldn't move an injured person. Thank goodness they didn't – it turned out that Tom had broken his back and later needed <u>major surgery</u> to put it right. First of all, however, he needed a <u>blood transfusion</u>, since he'd lost so much blood. He's still in <u>plaster</u>, and likely to be so for some time to come.

At about the same time, I developed a rash on my face. It turned out that I was <u>allergic</u> to the soap I was using. The doctor gave me some <u>cream</u> to rub on my face every evening and a prescription for <u>antibiotics</u>. I had to take a <u>dose</u> of three <u>pills</u> twice a day, but this did the trick and my skin is now clear.

1 cutting a body open in order to repair it ....

2 medicine or drugs used to improve a condition or illness ....

3 a substance you rub into your skin as a medical treatment ....

4 special vehicle used to take ill or injured people to hospital ....

5 a protective covering for a broken bone ....

6 equipment used to keep someone alive when they are very ill ....

7 small round pieces of medication which you swallow ....

8 medical operation in which a part of someone's body is put into another person's body ....

9 continuous treatment for patients who are very ill ....

10 medication that can destroy harmful bacteria ....

11 basic medical treatment given to someone as soon as they are hurt ....

12 reacting badly to something ....

13 measured amount of medication ....

14 process in which blood given by other people is put into another person's body ....

15 a very serious operation ....

20 Science

A Complete the chart. The words all end in -ist.

subject	person
1 science	*scientist*
2 biology	
3 chemistry	
4 physics	
5 zoology	
6 genetics	

B Find the first letter of the words connected with science. Write the words.

1 ....   6 ....

2 ....   7 ....

3 ....   8 ....

4 ....   9 ....

5 ....   10 ....

1 e h / o t / r y

2 d o / m h / e t

3 r a e s / c h r / e

4 y r o t / l a / a b o r

5 t / a a / d

6 r e p x / i e / m e n t

7 t s e t / t u b e

8 s t / r l / e s u

9 c s o r / o c / P e m i

10 p a s u / P t / a r a

C Complete the text with the words from B.

I have wanted to be a scientist ever since I read about Einstein and his
(1) .... of relativity. But at school, it was chemistry that I loved
most. We did an (2) .... most lessons – adding acid to a
substance in a (3) .... , that kind of thing – and then wrote it up
for homework. I loved the fact that it always had to be written up using the same
headings. First of all (4) .... – the equipment we had used;
(5) .... – how we had done the experiment; and finally,
(6) .... – what we had found out. It all seems a long time ago,
however! Nowadays, I work in a university (7) .... , where we are
doing (8) .... into fireproof textiles. I spend a lot of my time
looking through a (9) .... We store all the (10)
.... we collect on a computer. It's good to know that my work could
be useful in saving lives.

Test 2 (Units 11–20)

A The underlined words are in the wrong sentences. Write the correct word for each sentence.

1 Remember to take your <u>operation</u> twice a day. ....

2 We put the feather under the <u>apparatus</u> so that we could examine it. ....

3 We set up all the <u>microscope</u> the day before we did the experiment. ....

4 As a result of <u>civilisation</u>, humans have become more intelligent than any other animal. ....

5 People from the younger <u>evolution</u> all know how to use computers. ....

6 A professor at the university is doing some <u>medication</u> into the prevention of malaria. ....

7 My dad had a hip replacement <u>research</u> and now he can walk quite well again. ....

8 There's an exhibition on in London about the <u>generation</u> of Ancient Egypt. ....

B Look at the words in the box. Circle the words for people.

aborigine   ancestor   antique   celebrity   descendant   era   fix   geneticist
heir   junkie   mansion   millionaire   science   star   VIP

C Complete the text with the words in the box.

customs   ethnic groups   folklore   native
settlement   traditional   way of life   westernised

One of the (1) .... who live in the Arctic is the Inuit of Canada. (2) .... has been in small towns and villages mainly on the coast, where there is access to fishing. The Inuit (3) .... is based on hunting, which provides food and clothing. Nowadays people often use motorised vehicles, but their (4) .... means of transport were paddle boats and sledges pulled by dogs. One of their (5) .... is to eat caribou (a type of deer) – but today many people eat it with French fries and tomato ketchup! The Inuit are becoming more (6) .... They used to wear clothes made from fur, but today they buy them from factories. At school the children study English, but they use their (7) .... language, Inuktitut, at home. They also learn tales from Inuit (8) ....

D Complete the sentences with one word from both boxes.

| blood | drug | dry | first |
| hard | public | red | test |

| aid | carpet | drugs | eye | habit |
| humour | transfusion | tube |

1 Some people who once used .... are now clean.

2 Patients sometimes have to have a .... during major surgery.

3 My cousin used to have a .... , but he's no longer hooked.

4 In most workplaces, someone is qualified to give .... when there's an accident.

5 When our Canadian relatives come and stay, we roll out the ....

6 Hold the .... over the flame and notice what happens.

7 .... is funny in a way which is clever and not very obvious.

8 Members of the royal family are in the .... all their lives.

E Circle the correct words to complete the sentences.

1 You've got too much work – I advocate / sympathise with you. So have I!

2 How do you think the staff will reply / respond if ten people lose their jobs?

3 How will your friends overreact / react when you say you're moving?

4 My dad gestured / grimaced with pain after he fell and hurt his back.

5 Please sit up properly – don't slouch / stretch like that!

6 My boss raised / shrugged her eyebrows when I asked for a day off work.

7 My parents disapprove / object to the noise our neighbours make.

8 My little brother fidgets / folds all the time – he never sits still.

F Match the words in the box with the definitions.

| amazement | backlash | condemnation | delight | outcry | suspicion |

1 the feeling that you do not trust someone, even though you have no evidence for this   ....

2 feeling of very great pleasure, satisfaction or happiness   ....

3 strong criticism, because something or someone is unacceptable   ....

4 great surprise, almost impossible to believe   ....

5 sudden strong reaction against a recent development in society   ....

6 strong expression of anger and disapproval   ....

21 Money and debt

A Circle the correct words to complete the text.

I started my own business – a small clothes shop – about five years ago. At first the (1) <u>costs / debt</u> were very high – finding the right place and decorating it, and buying the clothes – but I managed to keep within the (2) <u>budget / interest</u> I had in mind. I'd hoped to make a profit fairly quickly and (3) <u>credit limit / invest</u> that in the business, as well as paying back the bank. But I've actually had to use up all of my (4) <u>savings / expenses</u> and borrow money from my brother to keep the business going, and now I find myself in (5) <u>broke / financial difficulties</u>. If things don't get better in the next three months, I'm going to have to declare myself (6) <u>bankrupt / in the red</u> and close the shop. In the meantime, I'm really going to have to (7) <u>economise / overdraft</u> – I'll have to get rid of my assistant and work in the shop myself all the time. Otherwise, there's no way I'll be able to (8) <u>cut back / make ends meet</u>.

B Complete the text with the other words from A.

I've just got my bank statement this morning and I see, to my horror, that my account is (1) _____ . I will have to pay (2) _____ on the money I now owe, although I can have an (3) _____ of £1,500 before the bank stops my cheques. However, I've nearly reached that limit. I've never been in (4) _____ like this before. I'm usually (5) _____ by the end of the month, but I pay my salary into my account and then I'm OK again. I've had a few (6) _____ recently, it's true – a new DVD player and my road tax. But I'm really going to have to (7) _____ – perhaps not buy the new digital camera I had in mind. I could use my credit card, but my (8) _____ is £2,000 and I couldn't pay the money back if I spent it. I need to win the lottery!

C Complete the sentences with some of the words from A and B.

1 If you have an _____ of £400, you have spent £400 more than you have in your bank account.

2 If you have a _____ of £400, you have £400 for a particular task.

3 If you owe _____ of £400, you owe £400 for borrowing money.

4 If you have a _____ of £400, you owe someone £400.

5 If you have a _____ of £400, you can spend £400 on your credit card.

6 If you _____ £400, you use £400 to buy property or shares in the hope that you will make a profit.

7 If you have _____ of £400, you have £400 in the bank for future use.

8 If you have _____ of £400, you have spent £400 for a particular purpose.

22 Religion

A Circle the places and underline the people.

(church)conventmonasterymonkmosque
nunpriesttempleworshipper

B Complete the sentences with the words in the box.

altar	believe	ceremony	faith	holy	pray	sacred	service

1 The Sunday evening .... will start at quarter past six.

2 Let us all .... for world peace.

3 The .... is usually in front of the east wall of a religious building.

4 This hill is .... to the local community.

5 Christians .... in and follow the teachings of Jesus Christ.

6 Some people get married in a registry office, but others prefer a religious

....

7 The origins of the Sikh .... go back to the fifteenth century.

8 The .... city of Mecca is the birthplace of Mohammed.

C Match words from A and B with the definitions.

1 to give thanks to or ask for something from a god   ....

2 building for Islamic religious activities and worship   ....

3 very religious or pure   ....

4 male member of a Buddhist or Christian community   ....

5 relating to a religion or considered to be holy   ....

6 table used in ceremonies in a Christian church   ....

7 a particular religion   ....

8 formal religious ceremony held at a particular time   ....

9 member of a female religious group which lives in
   a convent   ....

10 building in which monks live and worship   ....

23 Birth and death

A Circle the words in the box associated with birth.

bury   coffin   dead   deliver   expecting   fatal   foetus   funeral   grieve
labour   maternity   midwife   newborn   pass away   post-mortem
pregnancy   premature   terminal   mourners   unborn

B Complete the text with the words which you circled in A.

My sister Julie phoned last May in a state of great excitement. 'I'm
(1) .... a baby,' she said. She was only two months into her
(2) .... at this stage, so the (3) .... was no
more than two centimetres long. But she was really thrilled! After seven
months, Julie collapsed in the street and was taken to hospital. Although the
ambulancemen joked that they didn't want to (4) .... the
baby, we were concerned for the (5) .... child. Sure enough,
my sister went into (6) .... shortly after the accident and
was rushed into hospital. The (7) .... had everything under
control and Julie gave birth without any problems. I visited her next day in
the (8) .... ward and saw my (9) .... niece
for the first time. Although she was (10) .... , she still
weighed three kilos.

C Complete the text with the other words from A. Use the correct form of the verbs.

I know we will all (1) .... one day, but it's not nice when it
happens to someone you love. And it happened to my poor old grandfather last
week. Two months ago, he was told that he had (2) .... cancer.
But it was a (3) .... road accident that killed him, not his
illness. He was in a car crash, and when the ambulance arrived, was pronounced
(4) .... at the scene. A (5) .... showed that he'd
actually died as a result of a heart attack. My grandfather had already left strict
instructions for his (6) .... – he was a member of the Green
Party and wanted us to (7) .... him in a cardboard
(8) .... , rather than a wooden one. He also wanted the
(9) .... to celebrate his life rather than (10) ....
for him. What a wonderful man he was!

24 Art

A Circle the correct words to complete the text.

The (1) <u>artist</u> / sculptor Paul Cézanne was born into a wealthy French family and did not need to rely on selling his latest (2) collection / <u>picture</u> in order to live. This gave him great freedom and time to develop his skills. A story tells that he once made a man sit one hundred times for his (3) <u>portrait</u> / studio, and then abandoned the (4) masterpiece / <u>painting</u> because he was only pleased with the shirt. Cézanne's most famous (5) <u>landscape</u> / sculpture is of Mont Sainte-Victoire, a mountain near his home, which he painted several times. Flowers and fruit featured in much of his (6) abstract / <u>still life</u> work. Although Cézanne is  sometimes called the father of (7) contemporary / <u>modern</u> art, he obtained recognition only in the last years of his life. His first (8) <u>exhibition</u> / gallery wasn't held until 1895 when he was in his late-fifties.

B Complete the text with the other words from A.

Barbara Hepworth was born in 1903 and became interested in (1) .... as a young child. After attending the Royal College of Art in London, she won a scholarship to Italy where she learnt to carve marble. Her work soon became entirely (2) .... , not intended to look like or even suggest anything in particular. Hepworth's reputation as a (3) .... was first recognised in 1951 when her (4) .... *Contrapuntal Forms* was exhibited at the Festival of  Britain. She carried out many commissions for public places, but her life ended tragically in a fire at her (5) .... in St Ives, Cornwall, in 1975. In her will, she requested that her garden with its (6) .... of her work be open to the public. That is now run as part of Tate, St Ives, a (7) .... which displays 20th century and (8) .... works.

C Circle the correct answers.

1 A painter works in <u>a gallery</u> / <u>a studio</u>.

2 A living artist's work is <u>contemporary</u> / <u>abstract</u>.

3 A rich person could buy an artist's <u>collection</u> / <u>exhibition</u>.

4 A picture of an arrangement of objects is <u>a still life</u> / <u>a portrait</u>.

5 A landscape is the work of <u>an artist</u> / <u>a sculptor</u>.

25 Literature

A Match the underlined words with the definitions below.

I have loved books since a very early age. As a child, my grandfather used to read the children's classic *The Little Prince* to me until I knew it off by heart. I have always loved fantasy – 'Alice's Adventures in Wonderland' was the first book of this genre I came across.

Nowadays I probably read about two books a week. I love reading fiction, and just wish I had the imagination to create a story of my own. I usually have two books on the go at the same time – perhaps something light, something which isn't too complicated and makes great bedtime reading, and a non-fiction book which needs more attention. I love biographies, for example, and also travel writing, but nothing too heavy and academic. When I'm on holiday, I always take a crime thriller with a complicated plot, and try to work out who did what to whom before the end of the book – and the end of the holiday!

What don't I like? I would never choose a romance, mainly because the theme is often silly and sentimental. In Britain Mills and Boon is probably the biggest publisher of such books, and I'm proud to say I've never read one! And I'd rarely choose historical fiction over something contemporary. I read *A Journey to the Centre of the Earth* by Jules Verne at school, but haven't read any science fiction since – it's not my type of thing. Oh, and another thing, I mainly read prose – I like poetry when it's read aloud by someone with a decent voice, but not when I read it myself.

1 stories which are set in the past ....

2 story about love ....

3 a book with an exciting story, often about solving a murder ....

4 entertaining and easily understood ....

5 particular style of writing ....

6 company which produces books ....

7 books about imaginary characters and events ....

8 serious or hard to understand ....

9 books about real events and facts ....

10 books about an imagined future, especially about space travel ....

11 the things that happen in a story ....

12 piece of writing which is well-known, and of a high standard and lasting value ....

13 words arranged in lines, and chosen for their sounds and images ....

14 main subject of a book ....

15 language written in sentences and paragraphs ....

16 stories that are not based on reality ....

26 Leisure activities

A Label the activities with the words in the box.

amateur dramatics   darts   DIY   drawing   flower arranging
gardening   hiking   horse riding   jogging   knitting   martial arts
needlework   photography   pool   yoga

1 ....
2 ....
3 ....
4 ....
5 ....
6 ....
7 ....
8 ....
9 ....
10 ....
11 ....
12 ....
13 ....
14 ....
15 ....

B Complete the sentences with leisure activities from A.

1 I go .... after work most days. It's better for me than walking
and I'm not fast enough to run.

2 My dad loves .... He grows most of our vegetables as well as
lots of flowers.

3 I'm quite interested in .... I do karate once a week and I've
just started kung fu.

4 I go to a .... class twice a week. We do lots of gentle exercises
and it's great for relaxation after work.

5 My brother's got great eyesight, which is perhaps why he's good at
.... Also, he's got a very steady hand, which also helps when
he's aiming at the board.

6 I became interested in .... when I was at school and we did
A Midsummer Night's Dream.

27 Time

A Complete the sentences with *day* or *year*.

1 You go on your *annual* holiday once a _____ .

2 Your *daily* routine is what you do every _____ .

3 2004 was a *leap* _____ .

4 If you pay your bills *monthly*, you pay twelve times a _____ .

5 Some countries put the clocks *forward* in one half of the _____ and *back* in the other half.

6 If you have a *weekly* piano lesson, you have it every seventh _____ .

7 For some people, the afternoon is the best *time of* _____ .

8 The lightest *time of the* _____ in North America is *mid*-summer.

9 *Noon* is twelve o'clock in the middle of the _____ .

B Match the times of day with their definitions. Write the letters in the box below.

1 the hours of the morning after midnight   **a** *dawn*

2 the early morning when light begins to appear in the sky   **b** *dusk*

3 the time in the morning when the sun first appears   **c** *the small hours*

4 the late evening when it is not yet dark   **d** *sunrise*

5 the time at night when you last see the sun in the sky   **e** *sunset*

1 _____	2 _____	3 _____	4 _____	5 _____

C Complete the sentences with words in *italics* from A and B.

1 We put our watches _____ when we travel from Europe to America.

2 Summer is generally the hottest _____ .

3 I'm really tired because I only got home in _____ .

4 I have _____ travel insurance, so I don't have to pay each holiday.

5 There are twenty-nine days in February when it's a _____ .

6 Strictly-speaking _____ is 12 a.m, not 12 p.m.

7 I have a _____ bus pass which I buy every Monday morning.

8 One evening, when we were in Laos, we saw a beautiful _____ .

9 It is said that dusk is the most dangerous _____ to drive.

10 Some people buy a _____ newspaper on their way to work.

11 I heard a cock crowing outside the tent and knew it must be _____ .

12 We have _____ meetings on the first Monday of the month.

28 Quantities and amounts

A Put the letters in order and complete the words.

1 We've been to the ballet _d_ _ _ _ _ _ of times. (d o n s e z)
2 She asked him _ _ _ _ _ _ _ _ _ times, but he didn't do it. (c s t o u l e s n)
3 I've got _ _ _ _ _ _ _ _ of letters to write. (h r e u d s n d)
4 You'll find _ _ _ _ _ of things to eat in the fridge. (l o d s a)
5 There are _ _ _ _ _ _ _ _ of starving people in Africa. (m s i l i l n o)
6 There are _ _ _ _ _ _ _ queues for the toilets. (e e s n d l s)
7 I've got _ _ _ _ _ of things to do before I go on holiday. (p s e l i)
8 You'll have _ _ _ _ _ _ of opportunities to see the film again. (p l n y t e)
9 We discussed the plans on _ _ _ _ _ _ _ _ occasions. (n o s u e r u m)
10 I've written to _ _ _ _ _ _ of residents about the problem. (s c r e s o)
11 There were _ _ _ _ _ _ _ _ _ of fans at the football match. (t a n h s d o u s)

B Write the words from A in two groups.

word + *of* + noun   **word + noun**

dozens of times

C Circle the correct words to complete the text.

When I first came to London from Rome, I found it very hard. For a start, I knew
(1) a few / hardly any words of English. And at the language school I went to,
(2) few / several students spoke Italian. As a result, I felt lonely. After (3) a few /
enough days, however, things improved and I soon knew (4) enough / few useful
phrases to eat in a restaurant and buy things in shops. I also began to get to know
my classmates, and now I've got (5) hardly any / several friends.

D Answer the questions.

1 Which two words/expressions from C can you use with
uncountable nouns?

2 Most of the words from A mean 'lots of' or 'many'. Which
word means 'without a finish or limit'?

3 If you are 'short of' things, do you have enough of them?

4 Which word from C has the same meaning as 'hardly any'?

5 Which word from C has the same meaning as 'a few'?

29 Immigration

A Match the underlined words with the definitions below.

I used to work in Italy. I had both a <u>residence permit</u>, which allowed me to live there, and a <u>work permit</u>, which allowed me to work there. You could also apply for <u>citizenship</u> if you lived there for ten years (which I didn't). Because I lived there, I was able to renew my passport at the British <u>embassy</u> in Rome.

*IMMIGRATION
Entry on 1/6/05
6 months only*

During my time in Italy, I went to the USA to visit an Italian friend of mine who was travelling round the world. He had entered the country on a <u>tourist visa</u>, but had found work there. In reality, you needed a <u>green card</u> to work in the States, so he could have been <u>deported</u> if the authorities had found out that his <u>papers</u> weren't in order. But he didn't want to <u>emigrate</u>, only to stay there for a few months.

Since my return to Britain, I've been teaching ESOL (English as a second language) to groups of women. Many of them are <u>refugees</u> who had to leave their own country and crossed the <u>border</u> illegally. They have come to this country as <u>asylum seekers</u>, but the government has imposed limits upon <u>immigration</u> and will decide if these people have a genuine case, or are <u>economic migrants</u>, in which case they will be sent back home.

1 the legal right to be a citizen of a particular country ....

2 document giving a foreigner permission to work in the United States ....

3 official document that allows you to live somewhere ....

4 line that separates one country from another ....

5 the official building of a group of people who represent one country in the capital city of another ....

6 official document allowing you to work somewhere ....

7 forced to leave a country because you have no legal right to be there ....

8 people who move to another country in order to make more money ....

9 the process of entering a country in order to live there permanently ....

10 official stamp in your passport which allows you to visit a country ....

11 leave a country and go to live in another one ....

12 people escaping their country, often because there is a war or not enough food ....

13 foreigners forced to leave their own country who ask for protection from another country's government ....

14 official documents, especially ones which show who you are ....

30 Letter writing

A Read the first and last line of four letters. Match the words in the box with the letters.

Hi, Ian!	Dear Sir or Madam	Dear Ms Eyton	Dear Mum
Yours sincerely,	Love from,	Best wishes,	Yours faithfully,
Ian Lees	Ian	Pam	Pam Eyton

A

(1) ....

I'm writing to enquire whether you have any job vacancies during the summer months.

I look forward to hearing from you.
(2) ....
....

B

(3) ....

I'm writing in response to your letter of January 14th.

Please contact my secretary to arrange an appointment.
(4) ....
....

C

(5) ....

Thanks for your letter and the cheque you sent me.

Take care and keep in touch!
(6) ....
....

D

(7) ....

Just a quick note to say I'll be able to come to the meeting on Friday.

Let me know whether I need to give anyone a lift nearer the time.
(8) ....
....

B Answer the questions.

1 Two letters are formal and two are informal. Which ones are formal?

2 Which formal beginning do you use when you don't know the name of the person you're writing to?

3 Do you end formal letters with your first name and surname, or only your first name?

4 Which formal ending do you use when you know the name of the person you're writing to?

5 In letter D, do you think the two correspondents are colleagues or relatives?

6 In which letter could you also use the endings 'All the best' and 'Regards'?

A Circle the correct words to complete the sentences.

1 My mum goes to the Sunday morning <u>ceremony / service</u> at our local church.

2 We had to show our passports when we crossed the <u>border / embassy</u> into Canada.

3 We've had <u>hundreds / numerous</u> enquiries about the camera we advertised.

4 My friend was in <u>labour / pregnancy</u> for forty-eight hours before her daughter was born.

5 When we were in Chiang Mai, a <u>monk / nun</u> said he would show us around the monastery.

6 My grandparents had friends in Australia, so they decided to <u>emigrate / enter</u> there.

7 There's a shop in town with a range of <u>expecting / maternity</u> clothes.

8 The boys wanted to play football, but they couldn't find <u>enough / several</u> people to make up two teams.

B Complete the letter. Write one word in each space.

Dear Sir or (1) _____
My latest bank statement showed that I was £505.17 in the
(2) _____ . I dealt with this by transferring some of my
(3) _____ from another account. A week later I received a
further statement which showed that I had paid £3.85 (4) _____ on
this amount. My understanding was that I could have an (5) _____
of £1200, so I was surprised by this. Could you explain why this happened? I
have never been in (6) _____ to the bank before.
I look forward to (7) _____ from you.
Yours (8) _____ ,

Doreen Bolton

C Match eight of the leisure activities in the box with the equipment.

| darts DIY drawing hiking horse riding jogging knitting |
| martial arts needlework photography pool yoga |

1 _____ – boots, stick
2 _____ – needles, wool
3 _____ – paper, pencil
4 _____ – drill, nails
5 _____ – cotton, needle
6 _____ – camera, film
7 _____ – hat, whip
8 _____ – cue, ball

D **Complete the second sentence so that it has the same meaning as the first. Write one word in each space.**

1 I have a two-week holiday <u>once a year</u>.
I have a two-week .... holiday.

2 Most people in my office have lunch at <u>twelve o'clock</u>.
Most people in my office have lunch at ....

3 I get a telephone bill <u>every month</u>.
I get a .... telephone bill.

4 The year 2000 was a year <u>of 366 days</u>.
The year 2000 was a .... year.

5 We have a cup of tea <u>in the middle of the afternoon</u>.
We have a .... cup of tea.

6 Some farmers get up at <u>the time when the sun first appears</u>.
Some farmers get up at ....

E **Complete the dialogue with ten of the words in the box.**

> abstract   artist   crime   gallery   genre   heavy   historical
> masterpieces   non-fiction   portraits   publisher   studio

A: What are you reading at the moment?

B: *The Girl with the Pearl Earring* by Tracy Chevalier.

A: Isn't that the name of a painting?

B: Yes, the (1) .... was Vermeer. He lived in Holland in the
seventeenth century and painted a lot of domestic scenes and
(2) .... The book's about the model who sat for him in his
(3) ....

A: So, is the book a detailed work of (4) .... ?

B: No, it's not (5) .... reading at all. Nobody knows anything
about the girl, so the book is about what might have happened. I suppose
you'd say it's (6) .... fiction.

A: Is that your favourite (7) .... ?

B: No, not at all. I tend to prefer (8) .... thrillers. But I like
Vermeer's work. That's why I wanted to read the book.

A: Have you seen any of his work?

B: Yes, I saw three or four of his paintings in a (9) .... in
Amsterdam. He only painted about forty pictures, I think. But they're all
recognised as (10) ....

31 Ups and downs

A Circle the correct words and expressions to complete the sentences.

1 If you are <u>downbeat / upbeat</u> about something, you don't show or feel much excitement about it.

2 If you <u>downgrade / upgrade</u> something, you change it for a better one.

3 If something has <u>a downside / an upside</u>, it has a negative side to it.

4 If there is <u>a downturn / an upturn</u> in something, there is an increase in it.

5 If something is <u>a letdown / a turn-up for the books</u>, it is disappointing because it isn't as good as you'd thought it would be.

6 If you <u>have a downer / have your ups and downs</u>, a mixture of good and bad things happen to you.

7 If something is <u>downcast / up and running</u>, it is established and working.

8 If you are <u>down-at-heel / up-and-coming</u>, you are badly dressed or in a bad condition because of lack of money.

B Complete the sentences with the other words and expressions from A.

1 If you are .... , you are becoming more successful in a job.

2 If there is .... in something, there is a reduction in amount.

3 If you .... on someone, you don't like them.

4 If you are .... about something, you are full of hope, happiness and good feelings about it.

5 If you .... someone or something, you reduce them to a lower level or position of importance.

6 If something has .... , this is the good or pleasant part of it.

7 If you are .... , you are sad and without hope.

8 If you say that something is .... , you find it strange or surprising, usually in a positive way.

C Complete the sentences with words and expressions from A and B.

1 He hadn't worked very hard, but he still felt .... about how he'd done in the exams.

2 I worked all night in order to get the machine ....

3 Why do you .... on Paul? What's wrong with him?

4 Economy class is full, so we'll .... you to business class.

5 There's .... to earning more money – you pay more tax.

6 Her last book was much better – this one was a bit of ....

32 Phrasal verbs: getting in touch

A Complete the sentences with *in, off, on* or *out*. Use one word three times.

1 My credit card payment is due, so I want to *send* this cheque _____ today.
2 Don't forget to *copy* me _____ on that letter you're sending to Mr Morris.
3 I've written that kind of letter many times, so I was able to *dash* it _____ .
4 My flatmate moved out a year ago, but I still have to *send* _____ her mail.
5 I saw the bill and decided to *fire* a letter of complaint _____ immediately.
6 Our wedding is in July, so we want to *send* _____ the invitations in April.

B Complete the text with *back, in, off, onto, through* or *up*. Use two words twice.

I didn't feel well yesterday, so I decided to *phone* (1) _____ sick this morning. I managed to *get* (2) _____ to the switchboard alright, but then I got *cut* (3) _____ . I had to *ring* (4) _____ , and this time the operator was able to *put* me (5) _____ to my boss. Unfortunately, my boss wasn't very pleased about my news – some important visitors were coming after lunch. He asked me to *get* (6) _____ to him by twelve if I thought I could come in for two o'clock. If not, he would have to *get* (7) _____ another colleague and ask him to attend the meeting instead. My boss was so angry I thought he was going to *hang* (8) _____ on me.

C Complete the sentences with phrasal verbs from A and B. Use *it* or *them* where necessary.

1 If you telephone your place of work, you _____ .
2 If you write or draw something very quickly without putting much effort into it, you _____ .
3 If you send an application for a job by post, you _____ .
4 If you send something to a lot of different people or places, you
_____ .
5 If you connect someone to someone else by telephone, you
_____ .
6 If you contact someone, especially by telephone or letter, you
_____ .
7 If you make sure that someone receives a copy of a letter that you are sending to someone else, you _____ .
8 If you write a lettter quickly because you are angry, you _____ .

33 Phrasal verbs: sport and exercise

A Look at the photos. Complete the sentences with the names of five sports. Circle the phrasal verb in each sentence.

1 When you kick off in .... , you start a match.

2 When you knock up in .... , you practise for a short time before the start of a match.

3 When you tee off in .... , you start a game by hitting the ball for the first time.

4 When you knock your opponent out in .... , you hit them so hard that they fall and can't get to their feet again.

5 When you break away in .... , you move ahead of a group of people.

B Replace the <u>underlined</u> words with the phrasal verbs in the box. Write the verbs in the list below.

> burn off   call me up for   send me off
> tone up   try out for   warm up   work out

Five years ago, I was invited to (1) <u>compete for a place in</u> the local women's football team. I was really excited! The day before the trial, I decided to (2) <u>train my body by exercise</u> for an hour in the gym. Then, in order to (3) <u>make my muscles firmer, stronger and healthier</u>, I did some stretching exercises – I needed to be as fit and healthy as I possibly could. On the morning of the match, I had a large breakfast. I was sure I would (4) <u>use by exercising</u> a lot of calories during the game. Once I got to the ground, however, things didn't go according to plan. After sitting on the bench for the first half of the game, I was told to (5) <u>do gentle exercise to prepare for a sports activity</u> on the touchline. I'd been on the pitch for five minutes before the referee decided to (6) <u>make me leave the field because I had broken the rules</u>. He thought I'd pulled someone down in the penalty area. I wasn't surprised when they didn't (7) <u>ask me to take part in</u> the next match.

1 ....   5 ....

2 ....   6 ....

3 ....   7 ....

4 ....

34 Phrasal verbs: not doing things

A Complete the sentences with *off* or *out*.

1 You don't have to go to the party tonight. You can still *back* _____ if you'd prefer.

2 For years afterwards, he wanted to *blot* _____ the memory of the accident.

3 They'll probably *call* the match _____. The ground's far too wet.

4 He said he would do a parachute jump, but I think he'll probably *chicken* _____ !

5 I was too busy to sing in the choir every week, so I had to *drop* _____ .

6 I complained about the service and they tried to *fob* me _____ with some excuse.

7 The match isn't going ahead. The other team have had to *pull* _____ .

B Complete the sentences with *from, of, on* or *up*. Use each word twice.

1 You can't possibly *duck out* _____ going to the wedding. He's your brother, after all.

2 I'll be away when it's Jackie's party, so I'm going to *miss out* _____ it.

3 He offered me a free theatre ticket, but I decided to *pass* it _____ .

4 Can you think of a good excuse to *get out* _____ going to the meeting?

5 I know she's bossy, but don't *shy away* _____ telling her your views.

6 You promised you'd buy her a car. You can't *go back* _____ what you said.

7 I know you don't like him very much, but don't *stand* him _____ again.

8 You'll have to do something, Paul. You can't just *walk away* _____ the problem.

C Replace the underlined words with phrasal verbs from this page.

1 My sister used to <u>avoid</u> close friendships <u>because she was nervous</u>.

2 We've decided <u>not to take advantage of</u> the chance to go to the USA.

3 They had to <u>cancel</u> the concert because two members of the band were sick.

4 The shop tried to <u>persuade</u> me <u>to take</u> last year's model.

5 I can't <u>avoid remembering</u> those terrible events.

6 I didn't <u>fail to keep</u> my promise. I did what I said I'd do.

35 Idioms: how you feel

A Do the idioms in *italics* have positive (P) or negative (N) meanings?

1 Kim's been off school for a week, but she's *on the mend* now.   *P*

2 I'm feeling *under the weather*, so I'm staying in this evening.   ....

3 You must be *dead on your feet* after working all night.   ....

4 I've been given *a clean bill of health*, so I can start work again.   ....

5 He'll be *as right as rain* if he takes things easy for a while.   ....

6 I hear you got promoted. That should put *a spring in your step*.   ....

7 Joe's a bit *the worse for wear*, so let's leave him in bed.   ....

8 I've been gardening all day. I'm *ready to drop*.   ....

9 Jane's *up and about* now, but she hasn't been outdoors yet.   ....

10 I could do with a holiday. I feel *run-down* at the moment.   ....

11 You'll *catch your death of cold* if you go out without a coat.   ....

12 He seemed tired last night, but he's *full of beans* this morning.   ....

13 I feel *like death warmed up*. I'm going to stay in bed.   ....

14 He's *as fit as a fiddle* and never has a day off work.   ....

B Complete the sentences with idioms from A.

1 If you have .... , you walk energetically in a way that shows you are feeling happy and confident.

2 If you are .... , you have a lot of energy and enthusiasm.

3 If you are .... after an illness, you are well enough to get out of bed and move around.

4 If you are told that you will .... , you are being warned that you will become ill if you go outside when you're not wearing enough clothes.

5 If you are .... , your health is improving after an illness.

6 If you are .... , you feel ill, possibly after drinking too much alcohol.

7 If you are .... , you are very healthy.

8 If you are given .... , a doctor examines you and states that you are healthy.

36 Idioms: succeeding and failing

A Circle the correct idioms to complete the sentences.

1 If something *bears fruit / misses the mark*, it produces successful results.

2 If a plan *gets off the ground / goes pear-shaped*, it starts or succeeds.

3 If something *falls flat / works like a dream*, it works very well.

4 If something *goes from strength to strength / misses the mark*, it fails to achieve what it is intended to achieve.

5 If an attempt to achieve something or to tell a joke *bears fruit / falls flat*, it fails.

6 If something *comes to nothing / gets off the ground*, it doesn't succeed.

7 If a plan *goes pear-shaped / works like a dream*, it fails.

8 If something *comes to nothing / goes from strength to strength*, it becomes better and better or more and more successful.

B Match the sentence halves. Write the letters in the box below.

1 If you *make it big*,	**a** you won't be successful.
2 If you *draw a blank*,	**b** you don't make any mistakes.
3 If you *make the grade*,	**c** your relationship starts badly, often with an argument.
4 If you *fight a losing battle*,	**d** you become successful or famous.
5 If you *don't put a foot wrong*,	**e** you have produced something as a result of it.
6 If you *won't last five minutes*,	**f** you improve something a lot.
7 If you *work wonders*,	**g** you are unable to get information, think of something or achieve something.
8 If you *get off on the wrong foot* with someone you have just met,	**h** you succeed at something usually because your skills are good enough.
9 If you *have something to show* for your efforts or time,	**i** you try hard to do something when there is no chance of success.

1 .... 2 .... 3 .... 4 .... 5 .... 6 .... 7 .... 8 .... 9 ....

C Complete the sentences in your own words.

1 If you get off on the right foot with someone you have just met, ...

....

2 If something hits the mark, ...

3 If you have nothing to show for your efforts or time, ...

....

37 Idioms and metaphors: colour

A Complete the idioms and metaphors with the words in the box.

black   blue   green   grey   red   white

1 If you get a _____ mark, people think that something you have done is bad and they will remember it in future.

2 If you are as _____ as a sheet, you are very pale, usually because you are frightened or ill.

3 If a subject or problem is a _____ area, people do not know how to deal with it because there are no clear rules.

4 If something happens *out of the* _____ , it happens suddenly and you are not expecting it.

5 If you are _____ *with envy*, you wish very much that you had something that another person has.

6 If a statement or an action is *like a* _____ *rag to a bull*, it makes someone very angry.

B Complete the idioms and metaphors with five of the colours from A.

1 If you *have* _____ *fingers*, you are good at keeping plants healthy and making them grow.

2 If you say something *until you're* _____ *in the face*, you keep saying the same thing again and again but no one listens to you.

3 If you *catch someone* _____ *-handed*, you discover them doing something illegal or wrong.

4 If you *feel* _____ , you feel sad.

5 If *something is given the* _____ *light*, it is officially allowed to happen.

6 If you think facts and situations are _____ *and* _____ , you have a simple and very certain opinion about them.

C Complete the sentences with idioms and metaphors from A and B.

1 I hadn't spoken to Alice for ages. Then she phoned me _____ .

2 Susie didn't look well. She was _____ .

3 If you don't hand in your homework, that will be _____ against your name.

4 I was _____ when a friend of mine won a trip to Australia.

5 Sarah gets very angry about inequality in the workplace. When her boss said that she should make the tea every morning, it was _____ .

6 I don't know who's responsible for looking after the money. It's a bit of _____ .

38 Collocations: *big* and *small*

A Circle the correct word to complete the collocations.

1 Video shops are *big / large* business these days.
2 I usually only carry *little / small* change in my purse.
3 So, you're getting married? When's the *big / large* day?
4 How did you cut your *little / small* finger?
5 During the party, we had to make *little / small* talk with the other guests.
6 When it was my dad's 50th birthday, he didn't make a *big / large* deal of it.

B Complete the collocations with *big* or *large*. What is the opposite of these words? Write *small* or *little*.

1 Tom's a ....*big*.... boy now. It's his birthday soon.   ....*little*.... boy
2 The farm produces a .... *quantity* of milk.   *big* quantity
3 Our dog eats a .... *amount* of food.   *little* amount
4 How old is your .... *sister*?   *big* sister
5 His new job made a .... *difference*.   *little* difference
6 I bought a .... *number* of pens and pencils.   *big* number
7 My sister works for a .... *business*.   *big* business
8 I've hurt my .... *toe*.   *big* toe

C Complete the text with collocations from this page.

My friend Judy got married a couple of weeks ago. Weddings are
(1) .... these days, but Judy and her fiancé Robin didn't want to make a
(2) .... of it, so they invited only a (3) .... of people
– about twenty in total – to the registry office. They also didn't want any presents. Instead,
they asked each guest to give a (4) .... of money, not too much they
said, to one of three charities they had chosen. What a sensible idea!

When the (5) .... arrived, the weather was pretty awful. After the
ceremony, we went for a meal in an Italian restaurant. I sat next to Judy's
(6) .... Katy, who's only ten years old and really sweet. Unfortunately, she
managed to burn her (7) .... on a candle when she was reaching across
the table for some bread. Otherwise, the meal was lovely. When we went outside, the
weather had improved – and this made a (8) .... to everyone's photos.

In the evening Judy and Robin had a party for all their friends. Even though Judy works for
a (9) .... which makes computer parts, she knows a
(10) .... of people. I didn't know any of them, and I don't like making
(11) .... with strangers. So, I spent most of my time in the kitchen
helping Judy's mum with the (12) .... of food that was needed to
feed 150 people.

39 Collocations: *give* and *take*

A Match the sentence halves. Write the letters in the box below.

1 If you give someone advice,

a you say what you know about a particular situation.

2 If you take care of someone,

b you join with other people in it.

3 If you give evidence in court,

c you pay no attention to what this person says.

4 If you take control of a situation,

d you attempt it.

5 If you give a good impression,

e you keep this person safe from injury and illness.

6 If you take no notice of someone,

f you tell them what you think they should do.

7 If you give something a go,

g you have a positive effect on someone.

8 If you take part in an activity,

h you have the power to organise or direct it.

1	2	3	4	5	6	7	8

B Complete the sentences with the words in the box.

action   advantage   chance   details   hand   lift   pride   word

1 If you give someone a _____ to do something, you allow them to do it.

2 If you take _____ over a problem, you do something to solve it.

3 If you take _____ in something, you feel pleased and satisfied with what you have done.

4 If you give someone _____ of an event, you tell them about the time, place, cost, etc.

5 If you take someone's _____ for something, you accept what they say.

6 If you give someone a _____ , you give them a free journey in your car.

7 If you take _____ of something, you make good or full use of it.

8 If you give someone a _____ , you help them do something.

40 Confusing verbs (borrow/lend, etc.)

A Circle the correct verbs to complete the sentences.

1 Could I <u>borrow / lend</u> your pen, Roberto?

2 Can I <u>bring / take</u> my sister to your party?

3 I hope you didn't <u>damage / hurt</u> your mobile phone when you dropped it.

4 I'll see you outside the theatre. Don't <u>forget / leave</u> the tickets, will you?

5 Can you <u>lay / lie</u> the table? You'll find the knives and forks in the drawer.

6 My grandparents used to have a big house, but now they <u>live / stay</u> in a flat.

7 Did you <u>look / see</u> under the chair? It might have rolled under there.

8 Hurry up, or we'll <u>lose / miss</u> the train!

9 I think the cost of living will <u>raise / rise</u> very soon.

10 What time of day did they <u>rob / steal</u> the bank?

11 I didn't <u>say / tell</u> my friends I was going out with him.

12 My dad didn't <u>learn / teach</u> me to drive – my mum did.

B Complete the text with the correct form of the other verbs from A.

Some years ago, when I was on my summer holiday, I (1) _____ at a
campsite in Greece for a few days. One day I went to the beach with some other
campers. I put my money, passport, etc. into my small backpack and
(2) _____ it with me. I had a swim, then (3) _____ on the beach
under the hot sun. The others (4) _____ that they wanted to go
windsurfing, and I decided I'd like to (5) _____ . It was hard work – I could
just about (6) _____ the sail, but soon my arms began to
(7) _____ . I went back to where I'd (8) _____ my backpack, but
I couldn't (9) _____ it anywhere. Someone must have
(10) _____ it while I was windsurfing. My new friends (11) _____
me some money, which was kind of them. But I had (12) _____ my
passport too and had to go to the embassy the next day to get a new one.

C Complete the table.

infinitive	past tense	past participle
1 bring	....	....
2 leave	....	....
3 lay	....	....
4 lie	....	....
5 steal	....	....
6 teach	....	....

Test 4 (Units 31–40)

A Complete the sentences with words or expressions which include *up* and *down*.

1 It took ages to build the tunnel, but it's now been .... for ten years.

2 My dad's health isn't great. He has his ....

3 My cousin started his own small business a few years ago. At first, things went well, but recently there's been a bit of a ....

4 John's always late for work, but yesterday he was on time. That was a bit of a ....

5 At first the check-in clerk said the flight was full. Then she said she would .... us to business class. We were thrilled!

6 I've just been promoted at work. I've got a pay rise, but the .... is that I have to work longer hours.

B Circle the correct phrasal verbs to complete the sentences.

1 If you're angry with someone, you might <u>fire off an email</u> / <u>dash off an email</u>.

2 If someone leaves a message on your answer phone, you will probably <u>call them back</u> / <u>put them through</u>.

3 If it's your best friend's birthday, you <u>send off a card</u> / <u>send on a card</u>.

4 If you're cut off, you <u>phone in</u> / <u>ring back</u>.

5 If you need to communicate with someone, you <u>get back to them</u> / <u>get onto them</u>.

6 If you want to end a phone conversation, you <u>cut off</u> / <u>hang up</u>.

C Complete the sentences with the correct form of six of the verbs in the box.

catch	feel	get	go	lay	learn	lie	raise	rise	rob	steal	teach

1 The price of houses .... enormously over the last few years.

2 It took a long time for the plans to .... off the ground.

3 You .... your death of cold if you don't wear something warmer.

4 After my horse-riding accident, I had to .... flat on my back for four weeks.

5 This is delicious? Who .... you how to cook it?

6 My cousin's wallet .... from his jacket pocket.

Test 4 (Units 31–40)

D Circle the correct words to complete the text.

I hadn't heard from my parents for ages. Then suddenly, out of the (1) <u>black / blue</u>, my mum phoned and said they were going to come and (2) <u>look / see</u> me. I was only just up and (3) <u>about / off</u> after a nasty cold, so I wasn't too pleased.

The flat was a mess, and there was only a very (4) <u>little / small</u> amount of food in the fridge. But my best friend said she would give me a (5) <u>go / hand</u> with the tidying up. I took (6) <u>advantage / control</u> of her offer, and together we tidied the place up. I'd also (7) <u>lost / missed</u> my purse, but she said that was no (8) <u>big / large</u> deal. She would (9) <u>borrow / lend</u> me some money to do some shopping.

When the big (10) <u>day / minute</u> finally arrived, I was ready for my parents' visit. What a real (11) <u>letdown / upturn</u> when they phoned to say my dad was feeling under the (12) <u>rain / weather</u> and they wouldn't be coming!

E Complete the sentences with phrasal verbs. Use the correct form of the verbs in the box and prepositions.

break	burn	call	chicken	fob	knock	pass	send

1 Two players .... in yesterday's match for fighting.

2 My boss got into a fight and .... the other person ....

3 The Olympic champion .... from the rest of the athletes halfway through the race and went on to win.

4 How many calories do you .... in a marathon?

5 We're going climbing, but Anna will probably ....

6 Jane .... the chance to go skiing.

7 I .... the party because I was ill.

8 The shop assistant tried to .... me .... by saying they'd get the watch mended, but I wanted my money back.

F Underline the mistake in each idiom and simile. Write the correct word.

1 The doctor gave me a clean ticket of health. ....

2 I'm so tired I'm ready to fall. ....

3 On Sophie's first day at work, she didn't put a hand wrong. ....

4 I tell my brother not to use my mobile, but I'm fighting a losing war. ....

5 I tried out for the team and made the ground. ....

6 I was blue with envy when my friend won a car. ....

Answer Key

1 Describing character

A
1 *confidence*
2 consideration
3 courtesy
4 creativity
5 enthusiasm
6 flexibility
7 initiative
8 loyalty

B
1 determination
2 honesty
3 independence
4 intelligence
5 maturity
6 originality
7 patience
8 reliability

C
1 considerate
2 courteous
3 independent
4 creative
5 enthusiastic
6 flexible
7 confident
8 patient
9 honest
10 loyal
11 mature
12 reliable
13 determined
14 original

2 Describing appearance

A
1 old-fashioned
2 fashionable
3 neat
4 dowdy
5 flattering
6 crumpled
7 stylish
8 unflattering

B
1 over-dressed
2 elegant
3 clean-cut
4 frumpy
5 immaculate
6 glamorous
7 nerdy
8 under-dressed

C

positive	negative
fashionable	crumpled
flattering	dowdy
neat	old-fashioned
stylish	unflattering
clean-cut	frumpy
elegant	nerdy
glamorous	over-dressed
immaculate	under-dressed

3 What your body does

A
1 ache
2 burp
3 blush
4 hiccup
5 itch
6 shiver
7 sneeze
8 sniff
9 sweat
10 throb
11 tingle
12 yawn

B
1 blush
2 shiver
3 sweat
4 itch
5 yawn
6 sniff

C
1 Your nose can run when you have a cold.
2 Your heart can beat fast when you're excited.
3 Your eyes can water when you cut up onions.
4 Your stomach can rumble when you're hungry.
5 Your ears can pop when you go up in a plane.

4 How you feel

A
1 edgy
2 uncomfortable
3 tense
4 uneasy
5 anxious
6 jumpy

B
1 composed
2 distracted
3 restless
4 apprehensive
5 settled
6 expectant

C
1 settled
2 expectant
3 jumpy
4 apprehensive
5 uncomfortable
6 anxious
7 distracted
8 uneasy
9 edgy
10 composed

5 Animal types

A
1. species
2. insects
3. invertebrates
4. vertebrates
5. amphibians
6. reptiles
7. mammals
8. herbivores
9. domestic
10. carnivores
11. Wild
12. pet
13. predator
14. prey
15. omnivores
16. rare
17. endangered
18. human

B

crocodile	horse
carnivore	domestic
predator	herbivore
reptile	mammal
vertebrate	vertebrate
wild	

6 Working and not working

A
1. shift
2. working hours
3. clock on
4. clock off
5. overtime
6. sick leave
7. day off
8. get the sack

B
1. lunch break
2. flexitime
3. knock off
4. take time off
5. holiday allowance
6. maternity leave
7. take early retirement
8. part-time job

C
1. a teacher
2. a nurse
3. an office worker
4. a shop assistant
5. a mechanic
6. a waitress

7 Early childhood

A
1. high chair
2. pushchair
3. cot
4. nappy
5. bib
6. pram
7. dummy

B
1. pre-school
2. childminder
3. nappy
4. teething
5. dummy
6. thumb
7. pushchair
8. playground
9. nursery
10. high chair
11. babysitter
12. pocket money

C
1. dummy, thumb
2. babysitter, childminder
3. cot, pram
4. nursery, playground
5. bib, nappy

8 Friends and relationships

A
1. f
2. e
3. b
4. a
5. d
6. c

B
a. 4
b. 5
c. 2
d. 1
e. 6
f. 3

C
1. f
2. d
3. a
4. c
5. b
6. e

9 Being good or bad

A 1 good
2 good
3 bad
4 good
5 good

B 1 e
2 c
3 a
4 b
5 d

C 1 clumsy – bad
2 competent – good
3 inept – bad
4 hopeless – bad
5 skilful – good

10 How you say something

A 1 beg
2 confess
3 confirm
4 demand
5 insist
6 instruct
7 report
8 request
9 swear
10 urge

B 1 insisted
2 confirmed
3 demanded
4 begged
5 confessed

C 1 Gary instructed Mrs Harris to go straight back to the office.
2 He swore it wasn't him.
3 She requested that Paul send her an email.
4 He urged Steve not to drink and drive.
5 The police reported that there had been a sharp increase in drug-related crime.

Test 1 (Units 1–10)

A 1 leave
2 part-time
3 childminder
4 nappy
5 teething
6 off
7 break/hour
8 allowance
9 overtime
10 clock/knock

B

character	appearance
1 determined	dowdy
2 honest	elegant
3 loyal	immaculate
4 flexible	frumpy
5 reliable	neat
6 creative	glamorous

C 1 predator / wild
2 amphibian / vertebrate
3 domestic / herbivore
4 endangered / mammal

D 1 false
2 true
3 false
4 false
5 true
6 true

E 1 apprehensive
2 settled
3 distracted
4 clumsy
5 capable
6 useless

F 1 popped
2 blushed
3 swore
4 urged
5 lost
6 hung
7 ached
8 beat
9 insisted
10 confirmed

11 Reactions

A 1 b
2 d
3 e
4 f
5 c
6 a

B 1 outrage
2 thumbs up
3 dismay
4 suspicion
5 delight
6 amazement

C 1 outcry
2 welcome
3 astonishment
4 condemnation
5 shock
6 backlash

12 Opinions: for and against

A 1 approve
2 undecided
3 back
4 sympathise
5 in favour
6 advocate

B 1 behind
2 disapprove
3 take sides
4 object
5 in agreement
6 oppose

C

for	against
advocate	disapprove
approve	object
back	oppose
behind	
sympathise	
in agreement	
in favour	

13 Talking about history

A 1 antique
2 bygone
3 ancient
4 ancestor
5 heir
6 descendant
7 empire
8 era
9 century
10 evolution
11 generation
12 civilisation
13 prehistoric
14 medieval
15 historical

B 1 century
2 ancestor
3 prehistoric
4 ancient
5 empire
6 antique
7 civilisation
8 medieval
9 evolution
10 generation
11 heir
12 era
13 historical
14 bygone
15 descendant

14 The rich and famous

A 8.00 They haven't always been famous
8.30 At home in the Caribbean
9.00 Harvard House Hotel
9.30 The Simon Smith Show
10.00 Rebel Without a Cause

B 1 personality, star
2 a household name, world-famous
3 rise to fame
4 millionaire
5 mansion (house), limousine (car)
6 red carpet
7 in the limelight, in the public eye
8 icon

15 Cultures

A 1 aborigine
2 indigenous
3 tribes
4 customs
5 folklore
6 settlement
7 native
8 traditional

B 1 way of life
2 westernised
3 multicultural
4 ethnic groups
5 civil rights
6 discrimination
7 cultural identity
8 heritage

16 Body language

A 1 fidget
2 slouch
3 stretch
4 tut
5 sigh
6 grimace

B 1 cross your legs
2 raise your eyebrows
3 lick your lips
4 fold your arms
5 clench your teeth
6 shrug your shoulders

C 1 grimace
2 raise your eyebrows
3 sigh
4 clench your teeth
5 tut
6 slouch
7 shrug your shoulders
8 fidget
9 stretch
10 lick your lips

17 Humour

A 1 a *joke*
   b wit
  2 a black (humour)
   b dry (humour)

3 a pun
  b satire
4 a irony
  b punchline

B 1 f
  2 c
  3 e
  4 a

5 d
6 g
7 b

18 Drugs

A drug abuse
drug addiction
drug dealer
drug habit
drug overdose
drug trafficking

be on drugs
be high on drugs
be hooked on drugs
hard drugs
soft drugs
take drugs

B 1 junkie
  2 fix
  3 clean

C 1 hooked
  2 soft
  3 junkie
  4 dealer
  5 fix
  6 overdose
  7 habit/addiction
  8 clean

19 Medical treatment

A 1 operation
  2 medication
  3 cream
  4 ambulance
  5 plaster

6 life-support
  machine
7 pills
8 transplant
9 intensive care

10 antibiotics
11 first aid
12 allergic
13 dose

14 blood
   transfusion
15 major surgery

20 Science

A 1 *scientist*
  2 biologist
  3 chemist
  4 physicist
  5 zoologist
  6 geneticist

B 1 theory
  2 method
  3 research
  4 laboratory
  5 data
  6 experiment
  7 test tube
  8 results
  9 microscope
  10 apparatus

C 1 theory
  2 experiment
  3 test tube
  4 apparatus
  5 method
  6 results
  7 laboratory
  8 research
  9 microscope
  10 data

Test 2 (Units 11–20)

A 1 medication
  2 microscope
  3 apparatus
  4 evolution
  5 generation
  6 research
  7 operation
  8 civilisation

B aborigine
ancestor
celebrity
descendant
geneticist

heir
junkie
millionaire
star
VIP

C 1 ethnic groups
  2 Settlement
  3 way of life
  4 traditional
  5 customs
  6 westernised
  7 native
  8 folklore

D
1 hard drugs
2 blood transfusion
3 drug habit
4 first aid
5 red carpet
6 test tube
7 Dry humour
8 public eye

E
1 sympathise
2 respond
3 react
4 grimaced
5 slouch
6 raised
7 object
8 fidgets

F
1 suspicion
2 delight
3 condemnation
4 amazement
5 backlash
6 outcry

21 Money and debt

A
1 costs
2 budget
3 invest
4 savings
5 financial difficulties
6 bankrupt
7 economise
8 make ends meet

B
1 in the red
2 interest
3 overdraft
4 debt
5 broke
6 expenses
7 cut back
8 credit limit

C
1 overdraft
2 budget
3 interest
4 debt
5 credit limit
6 invest
7 savings
8 expenses

22 Religion

A

places	people
church	monk
convent	nun
monastery	priest
mosque	worshipper
temple	

B
1 service
2 pray
3 altar
4 sacred
5 believe
6 ceremony
7 faith
8 holy

C
1 pray
2 mosque
3 holy
4 monk
5 sacred
6 altar
7 faith
8 service
9 nun
10 monastery

23 Birth and death

A
deliver
expecting
foetus
labour
maternity
midwife
newborn
pregnancy
premature
unborn

B
1 expecting
2 pregnancy
3 foetus
4 deliver
5 unborn
6 labour
7 midwife
8 maternity
9 newborn
10 premature

C
1 pass away
2 terminal
3 fatal
4 dead
5 post–mortem
6 funeral
7 bury
8 coffin
9 mourners
10 grieve

24 Art

A
1 artist
2 picture
3 portrait
4 painting
5 landscape
6 still life
7 modern
8 exhibition

B
1 sculpture
2 abstract
3 sculptor
4 masterpiece
5 studio
6 collection
7 gallery
8 contemporary

C 1 a studio   **3** collection   **5** an artist
  2 contemporary   **4** a still life

25 Literature

A 1 historical fiction   **5** genre   **10** science fiction   **15** prose
  2 romance   **6** publisher   **11** plot   **16** fantasy
  3 crime thriller   **7** fiction   **12** classic
  4 light   **8** heavy   **13** poetry
        9 non-fiction   **14** theme

26 Leisure activities

A 1 horse riding   **9** needlework   **B 1** jogging
  2 flower arranging   **10** hiking   **2** gardening
  3 jogging   **11** photography   **3** martial arts
  4 DIY   **12** yoga   **4** yoga
  5 drawing   **13** pool   **5** darts
  6 amateur dramatics   **14** martial arts   **6** amateur dramatics
  7 knitting   **15** darts
  8 gardening

27 Time

A 1 year   **6** day   **B 1** c   **C 1** back   **7** weekly
  2 day   **7** day   **2** a   **2** time of the year   **8** sunset
  3 year   **8** year   **3** d   **3** the small hours   **9** time of day
  4 year   **9** day   **4** b   **4** annual   **10** daily
  5 year   **5** e   **5** leap year   **11** dawn
                         6 noon   **12** monthly

28 Quantities and amounts

A 1 dozens   **7** piles
  2 countless   **8** plenty
  3 hundreds   **9** numerous
  4 loads   **10** scores
  5 millions   **11** thousands
  6 endless

B word + *of* + noun
dozens
hundreds
loads
millions
piles
plenty
scores
thousands

word + noun
countless
endless
numerous

C 1 hardly any   **D 1** enough / hardly any
  2 few   **2** endless
  3 a few   **3** no
  4 enough   **4** few
  5 several   **5** several

29 Immigration

A 1 citizenship
  2 green card
  3 residence permit
  4 border
  5 embassy
  6 work permit
  7 deported
  8 economic migrants
  9 immigration
  10 tourist visa
  11 emigrate
  12 refugee
  13 asylum seekers
  14 papers

30 Letter writing

A 1 Dear Sir or Madam
  2 Yours faithfully, Pam Eyton
  3 Dear Ms Eyton
  4 Yours sincerely, Ian Lees
  5 Dear Mum
  6 Love from, Ian
  7 Hi, Ian!
  8 Best wishes, Pam

B 1 A and B
  2 Dear Sir or Madam
  3 first name and surname
  4 Yours sincerely
  5 colleagues
  6 D

Test 3 (Units 21–30)

A 1 service
  2 border
  3 numerous
  4 labour
  5 monk
  6 emigrate
  7 maternity
  8 enough

B 1 Madam
  2 red
  3 funds/money/savings
  4 interest
  5 overdraft
  6 debt
  7 hearing
  8 faithfully

C 1 hiking
  2 knitting
  3 drawing
  4 DIY
  5 needlework
  6 photography
  7 horse riding
  8 pool

D 1 annual
  2 midday/noon
  3 monthly
  4 leap
  5 mid-afternoon
  6 sunrise

E 1 artist
  2 portraits
  3 studio
  4 non-fiction
  5 heavy
  6 historical
  7 genre
  8 crime
  9 gallery
  10 masterpieces

31 Ups and downs

A 1 downbeat
  2 upgrade
  3 a downside
  4 an upturn
  5 a letdown
  6 have your ups and downs
  7 up and running
  8 down-at-heel

B 1 up-and-coming
  2 a downturn
  3 have a downer
  4 upbeat
  5 downgrade
  6 an upside
  7 downcast
  8 a turn-up for the books

C 1 upbeat
  2 up and running
  3 have a downer
  4 upgrade
  5 a downside
  6 a letdown

32 Phrasal verbs: getting in touch

A 1 off
2 in
3 off
4 on
5 off
6 out

B 1 in
2 through
3 off
4 back
5 through
6 back
7 onto
8 up

C 1 phone in
2 dash it off
3 send it off
4 send it out
5 put them through
6 get onto them
7 copy them in
8 fire it off

33 Phrasal verbs: sport and exercise

A 1 football – kick off
2 tennis – knock up
3 golf – tee off
4 boxing – knock (your opponent) out
5 athletics/running/a race – break away

B 1 try out for
2 work out
3 tone up
4 burn off
5 warm up
6 send me off
7 call me up for

34 Phrasal verbs: not doing things

A 1 out
2 out
3 off
4 out
5 out
6 off
7 out

B 1 of
2 on
3 up
4 of
5 from
6 on
7 up
8 from

C 1 shy away from
2 (to) pass up
3 call off
4 fob me off with
5 blot out
6 go back on

35 Idioms: how you feel

A 1 *positive*
2 negative
3 negative
4 positive
5 positive
6 positive
7 negative
8 negative
9 positive
10 negative
11 negative
12 positive
13 negative
14 positive

B 1 a spring in your step
2 full of beans
3 up and about
4 catch your death of cold
5 on the mend
6 the worse for wear
7 as fit as a fiddle / as right as rain
8 a clean bill of health

36 Idioms: succeeding and failing

A 1 bears fruit
2 gets off the ground
3 works like a dream
4 misses the mark
5 falls flat
6 comes to nothing
7 goes pear-shaped
8 goes from strength to strength

B 1 d
2 g
3 h
4 i
5 b
6 a
7 f
8 c
9 e

C 1 your relationship starts well
2 it achieves what it is intended to achieve
3 you have produced nothing as a result of it

37 Idioms and metaphors: colour

A 1 black
2 white
3 grey
4 blue
5 green
6 red

B 1 green
2 blue
3 red
4 blue
5 green
6 black, white

C 1 out of the blue
2 as white as a sheet
3 a black mark
4 green with envy
5 like a red rag to a bull
6 a grey area

38 Collocations: big and small

A 1 big
2 small
3 big
4 little
5 small
6 big

B 1 *big, little*
2 large, small
3 large, small
4 big, little
5 big, small
6 large, small
7 large, small
8 big, little

C 1 big business
2 big deal
3 small number
4 small amount
5 big day
6 little sister
7 little finger
8 big difference
9 small business
10 large number
11 small talk
12 large amount/
quantity

39 Collocations: *give* and *take*

A 1 f
2 e
3 a
4 h
5 g
6 c
7 d
8 b

B 1 chance
2 action
3 pride
4 details
5 word
6 lift
7 advantage
8 hand

40 Confusing verbs (*borrow/lend*, etc)

A 1 borrow
2 bring
3 damage
4 forget
5 lay
6 live
7 look
8 miss
9 rise
10 rob
11 tell
12 teach

B 1 stayed
2 took
3 lay
4 said
5 learn
6 raise
7 hurt
8 left
9 see
10 stolen
11 lent
12 lost

C 1 brought, brought
2 left, left
3 laid, laid
4 lay, lain
5 stole, stolen
6 taught, taught

Test 4 (Units 31–40)

A 1 up and running
2 ups and downs
3 downturn
4 turn-up for the books
5 upgrade
6 downside

B 1 fire off an email
2 call them back
3 send off a card
4 ring back
5 get onto them
6 hang up

C 1 has risen
2 get
3 will catch
4 lie
5 taught
6 was stolen

D 1 blue
2 see
3 about
4 small
5 hand
6 advantage
7 lost
8 big
9 lend
10 day
11 letdown
12 weather

E 1 were sent off
2 knocked ... out
3 broke away
4 burn off
5 chicken out
6 passed up
7 called off
8 fob ... off

F 1 ticket, bill
2 fall, drop
3 hand, foot
4 war, battle
5 ground, grade
6 blue, green

Word List

The words in this list are British English. Sometimes we give you an important American word which means the same.

1 Describing character

confidence /'kɒnfɪdənts/
consideration /kənˌsɪdər'eɪʃən/
courtesy /'kɜːtəsi/
creativity /ˌkriːeɪ'tɪvəti/
determination /dɪˌtɜːmɪ'neɪʃən/
enthusiasm /ɪn'θjuːziæzəm/
flexibility /ˌfleksɪ'bɪləti/
honesty /'ɒnɪsti/

independence /ˌɪndɪ'pendənts/
initiative /ɪ'nɪʃətɪv/
intelligence /ɪn'telɪdʒənts/
loyalty /'lɔɪəlti/
maturity /mə'tjʊərəti/
originality /əˌrɪdʒən'æləti/
patience /'peɪʃənts/
reliability /rɪˌlaɪə'bɪləti/

2 Describing appearance

clean-cut /ˌkliːn'kʌt/
crumpled /'krʌmpld/
dowdy /'daʊdi/
elegant /'elɪgənt/
fashionable /'fæʃənəbl/
flattering /'flætərɪŋ/
frumpy /'frʌmpi/
glamorous /'glæmərəs/

immaculate /ɪ'mækjələt/
neat /niːt/
nerdy /'nɜːdi/
old-fashioned /ˌəʊld'fæʃənd/
over-dressed /ˌəʊvə'drest/
stylish /'staɪlɪʃ/
under-dressed /ˌʌndə'drest/
unflattering /ʌn'flætərɪŋ/

3 What your body does

ache /eɪk/
blush /blʌʃ/
burp /bɜːp/
hiccup /'hɪkʌp/
itch /ɪtʃ/
shiver /'ʃɪvə/
sneeze /sniːz/
sniff /snɪf/
sweat /swet/

throb /θrɒb/
tingle /'tɪŋgl/
yawn /jɔːn/
your ears pop /jɔːr 'ɪəz ˌpɒp/
your eyes water /jɔːr 'aɪz ˌwɔːtə/
your heart beats /jɔː 'hɑːt ˌbiːts/
your nose runs /jɔː 'nəʊz ˌrʌnz/
your stomach rumbles /jɔː 'stʌmək ˌrʌmblz/

4 How you feel

anxious /'æŋkʃəs/
apprehensive /ˌæprɪ'hentsɪv/
composed /kəm'pəʊzd/
distracted /dɪ'stræktɪd/
edgy /'edʒi/
expectant /ɪk'spektənt/

jumpy /'dʒʌmpi/
restless /'restləs/
settled /'setld/
tense /tents/
uncomfortable /ʌn'kʌmpftəbl/
uneasy /ʌn'iːzi/

5 Animal types

amphibian /æmˈfɪbiən/
carnivore /ˈkɑːnɪvɔː/
domestic /dəˈmestɪk/
endangered /ɪnˈdeɪndʒəd/
herbivore /ˈhɜːbɪvɔː/
human /ˈhjuːmən/
insect /ˈɪnsekt/
invertebrate /ɪnˈvɜːtɪbreɪt/
mammal /ˈmæməl/

omnivore /ˈɒmnɪvɔː/
pet /pet/
predator /ˈpredətə/
prey /preɪ/
rare /reə/
reptile /ˈreptaɪl/
species /ˈspiːʃiːz/
vertebrate /ˈvɜːtɪbreɪt/
wild /waɪld/

6 Working and not working

clock off /klɒk ˈɒf/
clock on /klɒk ˈɒn/
day off /deɪ ˈɒf/
flexitime /ˈfleksitaɪm/
get the sack /get ðə ˈsæk/
holiday allowance /ˈhɒlədeɪ əˌlaʊənts/
knock off /nɒk ˈɒf/
lunch break /ˈlʌntʃ breɪk/
maternity leave /məˈtɜːnəti liːv/
overtime /ˈəʊvətaɪm/
part-time job /ˌpɑːt taɪm ˈdʒɒb/
shift /ʃɪft/
sick leave /ˈsɪk liːv/
take early retirement /teɪk ˌɜːli rɪˈtaɪəmənt/
take time off /teɪk taɪm ˈɒf/
working hours /ˈwɜːkɪŋ ˌaʊəz/

7 Early childhood

babysitter /ˈbeɪbɪˌsɪtə/
bib /bɪb/
childminder /ˈtʃaɪldˌmaɪndə/
cot /kɒt/
dummy /ˈdʌmi/
high chair /ˈhaɪ tʃeə/
nappy /ˈnæpi/
nursery /ˈnɜːsəri/

playground /ˈpleɪɡraʊnd/
pocket money /ˈpɒkɪt ˌmʌni/
pram /præm/
pre-school /ˈpriːskuːl/
pushchair /ˈpʊʃtʃeə/
suck your thumb /sʌk jɔː ˈθʌm/
teething /ˈtiːðɪŋ/

8 Friends and relationships
best friend /best frend/
childhood sweethearts /'tʃaɪldhʊd 'swiːthɑːts/
circle of friends /'sɜːkl əv frendz/
clique /kliːk/
fiancé(e) /fi'ɒnseɪ/
flatmate /'flætmeɪt/
friend of a friend /ˌfrend əv ə 'frend/
just (good) friends /dʒʌst 'frendz/
mutual friend /ˌmjuːtʃuəl 'frend/
old friend /əʊld 'frend/
pen pal /'pen ˌpæl/
peers /pɪəz/
school friend /'skuːl frend/
get to know (sb) /get tə 'nəʊ/
get on (with sb) /get 'ɒn/
(be) good friends (with sb) /gʊd 'frendz/
grow apart /grəʊ ə'pɑːt/
hang around (with sb) /hæŋ ə'raʊnd/
have a lot in common (with sb) /hæv ə ˌlɒt ɪn 'kɒmən/
introduce /ˌɪntrə'djuːs/
keep in touch /ˌkiːp ɪn 'tʌtʃ/
lose contact /ˌluːz 'kɒntækt/
make friends /ˌmeɪk 'frendz/
(be) on speaking terms /ɒn 'spiːkɪŋ tɜːmz/

9 Being good or bad
capable /'keɪpəbl/
clumsy /'klʌmzi/
competent /'kɒmpɪtənt/
effective /ɪ'fektɪv/
efficient /ɪ'fɪʃənt/

hopeless /'həʊpləs/
inept /ɪ'nept/
proficient /prə'fɪʃənt/
skilful /'skɪlfəl/ (US = skillful)
useless /'juːsləs/

10 How you say something
beg /beg/
confess /kən'fes/
confirm /kən'fɜːm/
demand /dɪ'mɑːnd/
insist /ɪn'sɪst/
swear /sweə/ (*past tense* swore;
past participle sworn)

instruct /ɪn'strʌkt/
report /rɪ'pɔːt/
request /rɪ'kwest/
urge /ɜːdʒ/

11 Reactions

amazement /əˈmeɪzmənt/
astonishment /əˈstɒnɪʃmənt/
backlash /ˈbæklæʃ/
condemnation /ˌkɒndemˈneɪʃən/
delight /dɪˈlaɪt/
dismay /dɪˈsmeɪ/
greet /griːt/
outcry /ˈaʊtkraɪ/
outrage /ˈaʊtreɪdʒ/
overreact /ˌəʊvəriˈækt/
provoke /prəˈvəʊk/
react /riˈækt/
reply /rɪˈplaɪ/
respond /rɪˈspɒnd/
shock /ʃɒk/
suspicion /səˈspɪʃən/
(get the) thumbs up (from sb) /θʌmz ˈʌp/
welcome /ˈwelkəm/

12 Opinions: for and against

advocate /ˈædvəkeɪt/
against /əˈgentst/
anti- /ˈæntɪ/
approve of /əˈpruːv əv/
back /bæk/
(be) behind (sb/sth) /bɪˈhaɪnd/
disapprove of /ˌdɪsəˈpruːv əv/
for /fɔː/
(be) in agreement /ɪn əˈgriːmənt/
(be) in favour of /ɪn ˈfeɪvər əv/
object to /ˈɒbdʒɪkt tə/
oppose /əˈpəʊz/
pro- /prəʊ/
sympathise /ˈsɪmpəθaɪz/
take sides /teɪk ˈsaɪdz/
undecided /ˌʌndɪˈsaɪdɪd/

13 Talking about history

ancestor /ˈænsestə/
ancient /ˈeɪntʃənt/
antique /ænˈtiːk/
bygone /ˈbaɪgɒn/
century /ˈsentʃəri/
civilisation /ˌsɪvəlaɪˈzeɪʃən/
descendant /dɪˈsendənt/
empire /ˈempaɪə/
era /ˈɪərə/
evolution /ˌiːvəˈluːʃən/
generation /ˌdʒenəˈreɪʃən/
heir /eə/
historical /hɪˈstɒrɪkəl/
medieval (also mediaeval) /ˌmediˈiːvəl/
prehistoric /ˌpriːhɪˈstɒrɪk/

14 The rich and famous

celebrity /sə'lebrəti/
household name /ˌhaʊshəʊld 'neɪm/
icon /'aɪkɒn/
(be) in the limelight /ɪn ðə 'laɪmlaɪt/
(be) in the public eye /ɪn ðə ˌpʌblɪk 'aɪ/
limousine /ˌlɪmə'ziːn/
luxury /'lʌkʃəri/
mansion /'mæntʃən/
millionaire /ˌmɪljə'neə/
personality /ˌpɜːsən'æləti/
red carpet /ˌred 'kɑːpɪt/
renowned /rɪ'naʊnd/
rise to fame /raɪz tə 'feɪm/
star /stɑː/
VIP /ˌviː aɪ 'piː/
world-famous /ˌwɜːld'feɪməs/

15 Cultures

aborigine /ˌæbə'rɪdʒəni/
civil rights /ˌsɪvəl 'raɪts/
cultural identity /ˌkʌltʃərəl aɪ'dentəti/
custom /'kʌstəm/
discrimination /dɪˌskrɪmɪ'neɪʃən/
ethnic group /ˌeθnɪk 'gruːp/
folklore /'fəʊklɔː/
heritage /'herɪtɪdʒ/
indigenous /ɪn'dɪdʒɪnəs/
multicultural /ˌmʌlti'kʌltʃərəl/
native /'neɪtɪv/
settlement /'setlmənt/
tradition /trə'dɪʃən/
tribe /traɪb/
way of life /ˌweɪ əv 'laɪf/
westernised /'westənaɪzd/

16 Body language

clench your teeth /ˌklentʃ jɔː ˈtiːθ/
cross your legs /ˌkrɒs jɔː ˈlegz/
fidget /ˈfɪdʒɪt/
fold your arms /ˌfəʊld jɔːr ˈɑːmz/
gesture /ˈdʒestʃə/
grimace /ˈɡrɪməs/
lick your lips /ˌlɪk jɔː ˈlɪps/
raise your eyebrows /ˌreɪz jɔːr ˈaɪbraʊz/
shrug your shoulders /ˌʃrʌg jɔː ˈʃəʊldəz/
sigh /saɪ/
slouch /slaʊtʃ/
stretch /stretʃ/
tut /tʌt/

17 Humour

black humour /ˌblæk ˈhjuːmə/
dry humour /ˌdraɪ ˈhjuːmə/
for a laugh /fɔːr ə ˈlɑːf/
have a laugh /hæv ə ˈlɑːf/
irony /ˈaɪərəni/
joke /dʒəʊk/
make fun of /meɪk ˈfʌn əv/
play on words /ˌpleɪ ɒn ˈwɜːdz/

pull (sb's) leg /pʊl ˈleg/
pun /pʌn/
punchline /ˈpʌntʃlaɪn/
satire /ˈsætaɪə/
tease /tiːz/
tongue in cheek /ˌtʌŋ ɪn ˈtʃiːk/
wit /wɪt/

18 Drugs

clean /kliːn/
drug abuse /ˈdrʌg əˌbjuːs/
drug addiction /ˈdrʌg əˌdɪkʃən/
drug dealer /ˈdrʌg ˌdiːlə/
drug habit /ˈdrʌg ˌhæbɪt/
drug trafficking /ˈdrʌg ˌtræfɪkɪŋ/
fix /fɪks/
hard drugs /ˌhɑːd ˈdrʌgz/

(be) high /haɪ/
(be) hooked /hʊkt/
junkie /ˈdʒʌŋki/
(be) on drugs /ɒn ˈdrʌgz/
overdose /ˈəʊvədəʊs/
soft drugs /ˈsɒft ˌdrʌgz/
take drugs /teɪk ˈdrʌgz/

19 Medical treatment

allergic /ə'lɜːdʒɪk/
ambulance /'æmbjələnts/
antibiotics /ˌæntɪbaɪ'ɒtɪks/
blood transfusion /'blʌd trænts͵fjuːʒən/
cream /kriːm/
dose /dəʊs/
first aid /ˌfɜːst 'eɪd/
intensive care /ɪn͵tentsɪv 'keə/
life-support machine /'laɪfsə͵pɔːt mə͵ʃiːn/
medication /ˌmedɪ'keɪʃən/
operation /ˌɒpər'eɪʃən/
pills /pɪlz/
plaster /'plɑːstə/
major surgery /ˌmeɪdʒə 'sɜːdʒəri/
transplant /'trænsplɑːnt/

20 Science

apparatus /ˌæpər'eɪtəs/
biologist /baɪ'ɒlədʒɪst/
biology /baɪ'ɒlədʒi/
chemist /'kemɪst/
chemistry /'kemɪstri/
data /'deɪtə/
experiment /ɪk'sperɪmənt/
geneticist /dʒə'netɪsɪst/
genetics /dʒə'netɪks/
method /'meθəd/
microscope /'maɪkrəskəʊp/

physicist /'fɪzɪsɪst/
physics /'fɪzɪks/
research /rɪ'sɜːtʃ/
results /rɪ'zʌlts/
science /saɪənts/
scientist /'saɪəntɪst/
test tube /'test tjuːb/
theory /'θɪəri/
zoologist /zu'ɒlədʒɪst/
zoology /zu'ɒlədʒi/

21 Money and debt

bankrupt /'bæŋkrʌpt/
broke /brəʊk/ (informal)
budget /'bʌdʒɪt/
costs /kɒsts/
credit limit /'kredɪt ͵lɪmɪt/
cut back /kʌt 'bæk/
(in) debt /det/
economise /ɪ'kɒnəmaɪz/
expenses /ɪk'spentsɪz/

(in) financial difficulties /faɪ'næntʃəl ͵dɪfɪkəltiz/
interest /'ɪntrəst/
in the red /ɪn ðə 'red/
invest /ɪn'vest/
make ends meet /ˌmeɪk endz 'miːt/
overdraft /'əʊvədrɑːft/
savings /'seɪvɪŋz/

22 Religion

altar /ˈɔːltə/
believe /bɪˈliːv/
ceremony /ˈserɪməni/
church /tʃɜːtʃ/
convent /ˈkɒnvənt/
faith /feɪθ/
holy /ˈhəʊli/
monastery /ˈmɒnəstəri/
monk /mʌŋk/

mosque /mɒsk/
nun /nʌn/
pray /preɪ/
priest /priːst/
sacred /ˈseɪkrɪd/
service /ˈsɜːvɪs/
temple /ˈtempl/
worshipper /ˈwɜːʃɪpə/

23 Birth and death

deliver /dɪˈlɪvə/
expecting /ɪkˈspektɪŋ/
foetus /ˈfiːtəs/
labour /ˈleɪbə/
maternity /məˈtɜːnəti/
midwife /ˈmɪdwaɪf/
newborn /ˈnjuːbɔːn/
pregnancy /ˈpregnəntsi/
premature /ˈpremətʃə/
unborn /ˈʌnbɔːn/

bury /ˈberi/
coffin /ˈkɒfɪn/
dead /ded/
fatal /ˈfeɪtəl/
funeral /ˈfjuːnərəl/
grieve /griːv/
mourner /ˈmɔːnə/
pass away /pɑːs əˈweɪ/
post-mortem /ˌpəʊstˈmɔːtəm/
terminal /ˈtɜːmɪnəl/

24 Art

abstract /ˈæbstrækt/
artist /ˈɑːtɪst/
collection /kəˈlekʃən/
contemporary /kənˈtempəri/
exhibition /ˌeksɪˈbɪʃən/
gallery /ˈgæləri/
landscape /ˈlændskeɪp/
masterpiece /ˈmɑːstəpiːs/

modern /ˈmɒdən/
painting /ˈpeɪntɪŋ/
picture /ˈpɪktʃə/
portrait /ˈpɔːtrət/
sculptor /ˈskʌlptə/
sculpture /ˈskʌlptʃə/
still life /ˌstɪl ˈlaɪf/
studio /ˈstjuːdiəʊ/

25 Literature

classic /ˈklæsɪk/
crime thriller /kraɪm ˈθrɪlə/
fantasy /ˈfæntəsi/
fiction /ˈfɪkʃən/
genre /ˈʒɒnrə/
heavy (reading) /ˈhevi/
historical fiction /hɪˈstɒrɪkəl ˈfɪkʃən/
light (reading) /laɪt/

non-fiction /ˌnɒnˈfɪkʃən/
plot /plɒt/
poetry /ˈpəʊtri/
prose /prəʊz/
publisher /ˈpʌblɪʃə/
romance /rəʊˈmænts/
science fiction /ˌsaɪənts ˈfɪkʃən/
theme /θiːm/

26 Leisure activities

amateur dramatics /ˌæmətə drəˈmætɪks/
darts /dɑːts/
DIY /ˌdiː aɪ ˈwaɪ/ (= do-it-yourself)
drawing /ˈdrɔːɪŋ/
flower arranging /ˈflaʊə əˌreɪndʒɪŋ/
gardening /ˈgɑːdənɪŋ/
hiking /ˈhaɪkɪŋ/
horse riding /ˈhɔːs ˌraɪdɪŋ/
jogging /ˈdʒɒgɪŋ/
knitting /ˈnɪtɪŋ/
martial arts /ˌmɑːʃəl ˈɑːts/
needlework /ˈniːdlwɜːk/
photography /fəˈtɒgrəfi/
pool /puːl/
yoga /ˈjəʊgə/

27 Time

annual /ˈænjuəl/
daily /ˈdeɪli/
dawn /dɔːn/
dusk /dʌsk/
leap year /ˈliːp ˌjɪə/
mid- /mɪd/
monthly /ˈmʌnθli/
noon /nuːn/
put the clocks back /ˌpʊt ðə ˈklɒks bæk/
put the clocks forward /ˌpʊt ðə ˈklɒks ˌfɔːwəd/
sunrise /ˈsʌnraɪz/
sunset /ˈsʌnset/
the small hours /ðə ˈsmɔːl ˌaʊəz/
time of day /ˌtaɪm əv ˈdeɪ/
time of the year /ˌtaɪm əv ðə ˈjɪə/
weekly /ˈwiːkli/

28 Quantities and amounts

a few /ə ˈfjuː/
countless /ˈkaʊntləs/
dozens /ˈdʌzənz/
endless /ˈendləs/
enough /ɪˈnʌf/
few /fjuː/
hardly any /ˌhɑːdli ˈeni/
hundreds /ˈhʌndrədz/
loads /ləʊdz/ (informal)
millions /ˈmɪljənz/
numerous /ˈnjuːmərəs/
piles /paɪlz/ (informal)
plenty /ˈplenti/
scores /skɔːz/
several /ˈsevərəl/
thousands /ˈθaʊzəndz/

29 Immigration

asylum seeker /əˈsaɪləm ˌsiːkə/
(cross the) border /ˈbɔːdə/
(apply for) citizenship /ˈsɪtɪzənʃɪp/
(be) deported /dɪˈpɔːtɪd/
economic migrant /ˌiːkənɒmɪk ˈmaɪgrənt/
embassy /ˈembəsi/
emigrate /ˈemɪgreɪt/
green card /ˈgriːn ˌkɑːd/
immigration /ˌɪmɪˈgreɪʃən/
papers /ˈpeɪpəz/ (informal)
refugee /ˌrefjʊˈdʒiː/
residence permit /ˈrezɪdənts ˌpɜːmɪt/
tourist visa /ˈtʊərɪst ˌviːzə/
work permit /ˈwɜːk ˌpɜːmɪt/

30 Letter writing

Dear Sir or Madam /dɪə ˌsɜː ɔː ˈmædəm/ (formal)
I'm writing to (enquire) /aɪm ˈraɪtɪŋ tə/ (formal)
I'm writing in response to /aɪm ˌraɪtɪŋ ɪn rɪˈspɒnts tə/ (formal)
Please confirm/contact /pliːz kənˌfɜːm / ˈkɒntækt/ (formal)
Yours faithfully /ˌjɔːz ˈfeɪθfəli/ (formal)
Yours sincerely /ˌjɔːz sɪnˈsɪəli/ (formal)
Hi! /haɪ/ (informal)
Just a quick note /ˌdʒʌst ə kwɪk ˈnəʊt/ (informal)
Keep in touch /ˌkiːp ɪn ˈtʌtʃ/ (informal)
Take care /teɪk ˈkeə/ (informal)
With love (from) /wɪð ˈlʌv/ (informal)
All the best /ˌɔːl ðə ˈbest/
Best wishes /ˌbest ˈwɪʃɪz/
I look forward to hearing from you. /aɪ lʊk ˌfɔːwəd tə ˈhɪərɪŋ frɒm juː/
Let me know /let miː ˈnəʊ/
Regards /rɪˈgɑːdz/
Thanks for your letter /ˌθæŋks fə jɔː ˈletə/

31 Ups and downs

down-at-heel /ˌdaʊnətˈhiːl/
downbeat /ˈdaʊnbiːt/
downcast /ˈdaʊnkɑːst/
downgrade /ˌdaʊnˈɡreɪd/
downside /ˈdaʊnsaɪd/
downturn /ˈdaʊntɜːn/
(have) a downer /ə ˈdaʊnə/ (informal)
letdown /ˈletdaʊn/
a turn-up for the books /ə ˌtɜːnʌp fə ðə ˈbʊks/
up-and-coming /ˌʌpəŋˈkʌmɪŋ/
up and running /ˌʌp ən ˈrʌnɪŋ/
upbeat /ˈʌpbiːt/
upgrade /ʌpˈɡreɪd/
upside /ˈʌpsaɪd/
upturn /ˈʌptɜːn/
have your ups and downs /hæv jɔːr ˌʌps ən ˈdaʊnz/

32 Phrasal verbs: getting in touch

copy (sb) in /kɒpi ˈɪn/
cut (sb) off /kʌt ˈɒf/
dash (sth) off /dæʃ ˈɒf/
fire (sth) off /faɪər ˈɒf/
get back (to sb) /ɡet ˈbæk/
get onto (sb) /ɡet ˈɒntuː/
get through /ɡet ˈθruː/
hang up /hæŋ ˈʌp/
phone in /fəʊn ˈɪn/
put (sb) through /pʊt ˈθruː/
ring back /rɪŋ ˈbæk/
send (sth) off /send ˈɒf/
send (sth) on /send ˈɒn/
send (sth) out /send ˈaʊt/

33 Phrasal verbs: sport and exercise

break away /breɪk əˈweɪ/
burn off /bɜːn ˈɒf/
call (sb) up (for) /kɔːl ˈʌp/
kick off /kɪk ˈɒf/
knock (sb) out /nɒk ˈaʊt/
knock up /nɒk ˈʌp/
send (sb) off /send ˈɒf/
tee off /tiː ˈɒf/
tone up (muscles) /təʊn ˈʌp/
try out (for) /traɪ ˈaʊt/
warm up /wɔːm ˈʌp/
work out /wɜːk ˈaʊt/

34 Phrasal verbs: not doing things

back out /bæk 'aʊt/
blot (sth) out /blɒt 'aʊt/ (informal)
call (sth) off /kɔːl 'ɒf/
chicken out (informal) /ˌtʃɪkɪn 'aʊt/
drop out /drɒp 'aʊt/
duck out of /dʌk 'aʊt əv/ (informal)
fob (sb) off /fɒb 'ɒf/ (informal)
get out of /get 'aʊt əv/
go back on /gəʊ 'bæk ɒn/
miss out (on) /mɪs 'aʊt/
pass (sth) up /pɑːs 'ʌp/
pull out /pʊl 'aʊt/
shy away from /ʃaɪ ə'weɪ frəm/
stand (sb) up /stænd 'ʌp/ (informal)
walk away from /wɔːk ə'weɪ frəm/

35 Idioms: how you feel

a clean bill of health /ə ˌkliːn bɪl əv 'helθ/
as fit as a fiddle /əz ˌfɪt əz ə 'fɪdl/
as right as rain /əz ˌraɪt əz 'reɪn/
(be) dead on your feet /ˌded ɒn jɔː 'fiːt/
(be) full of beans /ˌfʊl əv 'biːnz/
(be) on the mend /ɒn ðə 'mend/
(be) ready to drop /ˌredi tə 'drɒp/
(be) the worse for wear /ðə ˌwɜːs fə 'weə/
(be) under the weather /ˌʌndə ðə 'weðə/
(be) up and about /ˌʌp ənd ə'baʊt/
catch your death (of cold) /ˌkætʃ jɔː 'deθ/
feel like death warmed up /fiːl laɪk ˌdeθ wɔːmd 'ʌp/ (US = feel like death warmed over)
feel run-down /fiːl rʌn'daʊn/
have a spring in your step /hæv ə 'sprɪŋ ɪn jɔː ˌstep/

36 Idioms: succeeding and failing

bear fruit /beə 'fruːt/
draw a blank /ˌdrɔː ə 'blæŋk/
come to nothing /ˌkʌm tə 'nʌθɪŋ/
fall flat /fɔːl 'flæt/
fight a losing battle /faɪt ə ˌluːzɪŋ 'bætl/
get off the ground /get ɒf ðə 'graʊnd/
get off on the right foot /get ˌɒf ɒn ðə raɪt 'fʊt/
get off on the wrong foot /get ˌɒf ɒn ðə rɒŋ 'fʊt/
go from strength to strength /gəʊ frəm ˌstreŋkθ tə 'streŋkθ/
go pear-shaped /gəʊ 'peəʃeɪpt/
have nothing to show for (sth) /hæv ˌnʌθɪŋ tə 'ʃəʊ fə/
have something to show for (sth) /hæv ˌsʌmpθɪŋ tə 'ʃəʊ fə/
hit the mark /ˌhɪt ðə 'mɑːk/
make it big /ˌmeɪk ɪt 'bɪg/
make the grade /ˌmeɪk ðə 'greɪd/
miss the mark /ˌmɪs ðə 'mɑːk/
not last five minutes /nɒt ˌlɑːst faɪv 'mɪnɪts/
not put a foot wrong /nɒt pʊt ə ˌfʊt 'rɒŋ/
work like a dream /ˌwɜːk laɪk ə 'driːm/
work wonders /wɜːk 'wʌndəz/

37 Idioms and metaphors: colour

a black mark /ə ˌblæk 'mɑːk/
a grey area /ə 'greɪ ˌeəriə/
as white as a sheet /əz ˌwaɪt əz ə 'ʃiːt/
(be) black and white /blæk ənd 'waɪt/
catch (sb) red-handed /ˌkætʃ red'hændɪd/
feel blue /fiːl 'bluː/
give (sth) the green light /gɪv ðə ˌgriːn 'laɪt/
green with envy /ˌgriːn wɪð 'envi/
have green fingers /hæv griːn 'fɪŋgəz/
like a red rag to a bull /laɪk ə red ˌræg tuː ə 'bʊl/
out of the blue /aʊt əv ðə 'bluː/
until you're blue in the face /əntɪl jɔː ˌbluː ɪn ðə 'feɪs/

38 Collocations: *big* and *small*

a big boy /ə bɪg 'bɔɪ/
a little boy /ə lɪtl 'bɔɪ/
big business /bɪg 'bɪznɪs/
a large business /ə lɑːdʒ 'bɪznɪs/
a small business /ə smɔːl 'bɪznɪs/
small change /ˌsmɔːl 'tʃeɪndʒ/
the big day /ðə ˌbɪg 'deɪ/
a big difference /ə ˌbɪg 'dɪfərənts/
a small difference /ə ˌsmɔːl 'dɪfərənts/
a big deal /ə ˌbɪg 'diːl/
your little finger /jɔː ˌlɪtl 'fɪŋgə/
big sister /ˌbɪg 'sɪstə/
little sister /ˌlɪtl 'sɪstə/
small talk /'smɔːl ˌtɔːk/
your big toe /jɔː ˌbɪg 'təʊ/
your little toe /jɔː ˌlɪtl 'təʊ/
a large amount /ə ˌlɑːdʒ ə'maʊnt/
a large number of (sth) /ə ˌlɑːdʒ 'nʌmbər əv/
a large quantity /ə ˌlɑːdʒ 'kwɒntəti/
a small amount /ə ˌsmɔːl ə'maʊnt/
a small number of (sth) /ə ˌsmɔːl 'nʌmbər əv/
a small quantity /ə ˌsmɔːl 'kwɒntəti/

39 Collocations: *give* and *take*

give (sb) advice /gɪv əd'vaɪs/
give (sb) a chance /gɪv ə 'tʃɑːnts/
give details /gɪv 'diːteɪlz/
give evidence /gɪv 'evɪdənts/
give (sb) a go /gɪv ə 'gəʊ/
give (sb) a hand /gɪv ə 'hænd/
give an impression /gɪv ən ɪm'preʃən/
give (sb) a lift /gɪv ə 'lɪft/
take action /teɪk 'ækʃən/
take advantage (of sth) /teɪk əd'vɑːntɪdʒ/
take care /teɪk 'keə/
take control /teɪk kən'trəʊl/
take no notice /teɪk nəʊ 'nəʊtɪs/
take part /teɪk 'pɑːt/
take pride /teɪk 'praɪd/
take (sb's) word (for sth) /teɪk 'wɜːd/

40 Confusing verbs
borrow /ˈbɒrəʊ/
bring /brɪŋ/ (*past tense & past participle* brought)
damage /ˈdæmɪdʒ/
forget /fəˈget/ (*past tense* forgot; *past participle* forgotten)
hurt /hɜːt/ (*past tense & past participle* hurt)
lay /leɪ/ (*past tense & past participle* laid)
learn /lɜːn/ (*past tense & past participle* learnt)
leave /liːv/ (*past tense & past participle* left)
lend /lend/ (*past tense & past participle* lent)
lie /laɪ/ (*past tense* lay; *past participle* lain)
live /lɪv/
look /lʊk/
lose /luːz/ (*past tense & past participle* lost)
miss /mɪs/
raise /reɪz/
rise /raɪz/ (*past tense* rose; *past participle* risen)
rob /rɒb/
say /seɪ/ (*past tense & past participle* said)
see /siː/ (*past tense* saw; *past participle* seen)
stay /steɪ/
steal /stiːl/ (*past tense* stole; *past participle* stolen)
take /teɪk/ (*past tense* took; *past participle* taken)
teach /tiːtʃ/ (*past tense & past participle* taught)
tell /tel/ (*past tense & past participle* told)

Acknowledgements

We are very grateful to all the schools, institutions, teachers and students around the world who either piloted or commented on the material:

Guitar Chou, Taiwan
Ludmila Gorodatskaya, Russia
Magdalena Kijak, Poland
Andrew Maggs, Japan

I would like to thank Martine Walsh of Cambridge University Press for her help, guidance and support during the writing of this series. My thanks also to Ruth Carim for her excellent proofreading.

The publishers would like to thank the following for permission to reproduce photographs:
p.10t Alamy (Gary Cook), p.10b (Adrian Sherratt); p.14tl Getty Images (John Kelly), p.14br (Greg Ceo); p.21 Corbis (Bettmann); p.22 (Tom Kidd); p.33b (Peter Barritt), p.33t (Self-Portrait, 1880 by Paul Cezanne/Photo Alexander Burkatovski); p.44tl (Reuters), p.44tc (S.Carmona), p.44cr (Charles W.Luzier/Reuters), p.44tr Action Plus (Glyn Kirk), p.44br (Fredrik Skold).

Photographs supplied by Pictureresearch.co.uk

Vocabulary in Practice

	SBN-10	SBN-13
Level 1 Beginner	0521 010802	978 0521 010801
Level 2 Elementary	0521 010829	978 0521 010825
Level 3 Pre-intermediate	0521 753759	978 0521 753753
Level 4 Intermediate	0521 753767	978 0521 753760
Level 5 Intermediate to upper-intermediate	0521 601258	978 0521 601252
Level 6 Upper-intermediate	0521 601266	978 0521 601269

Grammar in Practice

	SBN-10	SBN-13
Level 1 Beginner	0521 665760	978 0521 665766
Level 2 Elementary	0521 665663	978 0521 665667
Level 3 Pre-intermediate	0521 540410	978 0521 540414
Level 4 Intermediate	0521 540429	978 0521 540421
Level 5 Intermediate to upper-intermediate	0521 618282	978 0521 618281
Level 6 Upper-intermediate	0521 618290	978 0521 618298